DATE DUE

Freneau's Published Prose:
A Bibliography

by

Philip Marsh

The Scarecrow Press, Inc.

Metuchen, N.J.   1970

The Scarecrow Author Bibliographies Series

Bibliographies of the following authors are forthcoming:

Table of Contents

Introduction

The Prose of Philip Freneau,[1] a selection of some 170 items, has aroused interest in a bibliography of all Freneau's prose, as a guide to reference and research. The present list includes titles of over 1100 pieces and over 300 pseudonyms, items being designated "certain" (no asterisk) and "probable" (as terisk). Nearly all the essay-size items' titles are here. Titles are supplied, in parenthesis, when absent, and the omissions are mostly short editorials and short editorial introductions.

There have been four Freneau bibliographies--one each by Pattee,[2] Paltsits,[3] and Leary,[4] and the Freneau section in Blanck's Bibliography of American Literature[5]--but none of these deal exclusively with his prose. Leary listed both poetry and prose pieces, but omitted some authentic essays and all the uncertain ones, though often very probably Freneau's. Blanck, like Paltsits, has made no attempt to record the individual prose writings, though many contain poems. In the present compilation, the "probable" items might be called "uncertain"; but most are almost certainly by Freneau, and their omission would eliminate a very important area of his work. Some might be called "nearly probable", "strongly possible", or "almost sure" --but all are characteristic.

Scope of this Work

It has been the intent to include all prose published in the author's lifetime, except for very short editorials and brief introductions to other pieces, along with items unpublished then but appearing later, separately. In general, his letters are omitted because they deserve separate treatment. No special attempt has been made to list the reprints of items beyond the first publication, though some are mentioned. Except for those in the Cyclopaedia of American Literature (1855), the author has not tried to include the reappearance of essays in anthologies.

The "certains" are ascribed by appearance in Freneau's collections;[6] his markings in his personal file of The Freeman's Journal;[7] the use of his name or initials or surname letters as signatures;[8] an assumption of his authorship of editorials, book reviews, and translations in papers he edited or liberally contributed to, if unsigned, unquoted, unascribed, and definitely in his manner; and by relationships to previously ascribed works.[9] In the Tomo Cheeki Essays, there is another sort of evidence; never collected, they originated in a tale of Tomo in the Miscellaneous Works; then essays by "Opay Mico" began in the Daily Advertiser, which Freneau was helping edit; next, most of these reappeared as by "Tomo Cheeki", in his Jersey Chronicle, to be republished in his Time Piece. There is a clear line of authorship-editorship in the series.

Editorials, Reviews, Translations

Editorials in oldtime newspapers were usually unsigned, often untitled, or mixed with news as running comments on it. Long editorials appeared separately, usually unsigned. Sometimes Freneau titled them, "Thoughts", "Reflections", etc. As these are obvious editorials, they are rated certain ascriptions because Freneau was the editor.

Book reviews were usually unsigned. Translations were also usually unsigned, unquoted, and unascribed. Both

6

reviews and translations are here considered byproducts of editorial writing; there were then no signs of freelance reviewers or writers on any subject, except interested contributors. Freneau also used fillers--unsigned and unascribe often descriptions of faraway places or people. They often appear to be paraphrases, perhaps partly copied. Some-- like "Shrewsbury" (NG, July 14, 1792)--were evidently from his own personal experience and observation.

Editorials in The Freeman's Journal, when by the owner, Francis Bailey, were signed by him. His style, bland and unliterary, can never be mistaken for Freneau's, which is sharp and literary. During Freneau's assistant editorship--August, 1781 to September, 1782--except for signed announcements, Bailey apparently wrote no editorials. After Freneau left, editorials all but vanished from the Journal. So it is assumed that during his stay the editorials were his, as by style they seem to be.

Contributions

Letters by "contributors", with characteristic pseudonyms and in Freneau's style, are considered "probable". The line between certain and probable is often so thin as to be almost invisible. Some of these contributions are obviously editorials, faintly disguised. There were contributions by others, but their styles are different.

Communications and Correspondents

Post-Revolutionary American editors treated "communications" and "correspondents" loosely--and Freneau was no exception. If a letter had a signature, it appeared without quotation marks. If it was partly quoted, that part was enclosed in marks. But it was often used as a starting point from which to editorialize, and was put under "Communications" with a casual "says a correspondent", or under "From a Correspondent". In most such cases, the contributor (if he existed) was not quoted directly; and what followed was in Freneau's style. Perhaps the practice began by paraphrasing the letter, whence it verged into the use of its idea as a subject for an essay. In Fenno's Gazette of the United States and Freneau's National Gazette, such headings usually meant an editorial. And sometimes, apparently, the editor had no qualms about references, and used the column freely for his own ideas. But there is a difference in matter under "Original Communications", which generally sounds as if written by someone else; yet it also must be suspected--for, after a quoted paragraph, we may find an editorial addition.

Separate Editorials

In 1792 Freneau, enraged at Fenno's treatment of quotations, may have thought his rival was cheating in "contributions", and so began contributing to the National Gazette under pseudonyms.

As time wore on, the combatants became hardened to battle. Freneau lost his temper to Feds in general and Fenno in particular. Now he evidently adopted the practice of filling space with his own material under a variety of pen names. There is no other common sense way to explain why so many letters that appeared in the National Gazette were in his style and advocated his ideas, yet were signed with fictitious names. There is little reason to think Fenno went so far; he was not much impelled to express himself, and

wrote little. His son, the hot-tempered John Ward Fenno,
however, may have been the author of many Freneau-rousing
items.

Probable Ascriptions

Circumstances, ideas, style--one is hardly enough to
justify an ascription, except where the style is exceptional.
But when all of these coincide, there is sound reason for
ascribing an item as "probable".

Circumstances indicating that Freneau could or would
have contributed at a particular time to a particular news-
paper, on a favorite subject, are present in nearly all the
"probables" here. Usually he was editing or contributing or
both. In other instances the style-content resemblances to
his known work are strong; and he was "available", as far
as is known. The many political letters in the National
Gazette of 1792-1793, especially from May to October, when
most of his congressional friends (and contributors) were
away, in the very style of his editorials and known essays,
appeared under conditions forcing a verdict of "probably his".
In the Aurora of 1799 to 1801, when he was writing the
Slender Letters, other essays in the same or a recognizably
Freneau style also appeared there.[10] Such are the "Scaevola"
essay (August 13, 1799) and "Refugee" (November 14, 1799).
A slightly doubtful example as to the circumstances is the
"Bunker" series in the Aurora of 1804. These essays are
almost sheer duplication, with small variations, of the
Slender Letters. The resemblance is so close that a
"probable" ascription is forced, and the temptation is nearly
irresistible to make it "certain". But we have no evidence
that Freneau was in Philadelphia then, though he often went
there; and there is no evidence that he was away.

9

Ideas

Freneau's ideas are often Rousseauistic, radically democratic--primitivism, condemnation of civilization; hatred of war, duelling, monarchy, tyranny, Britain; love of democracy, common men's rights, peace, justice, France. He believed in life's tenuousness, sleep as a form of death, the need for reason. He criticized cruelty to animals and servants, aristocracy, "great" men, ambition, display, and education for acquiring wealth. He had faith in deism, benevolence, brotherhood, and rural life. He noted the folly of fashion, the soporific effects of custom, and life's continual change and activity. He regretted the futility of literary aspirations, the hardships of debtors and teachers, the tragedy of the Indian, the whites' pride in their "superiority", and the childish desire for novelty. He ridiculed Tories, sentimental novels, law and lawyers, and history. He damned avarice, pomposity, and pride. These ideas were, of course, not original. But it was unusual to find, in Freneau's America, one writer advocating or opposing them all.

Style

Freneau's style is very individual, easy to spot among essays of his day. There is seldom any doubt that a characteristic item could have been his. Others used one or two of his "tricks"--but almost without exception, no other American newspaper writer of the time used such an individualistic cluster of habits--Latinisms (indubitable, elucidate). Latin-Greek allusions and quotations (Homer, Horace, Virgil); English or French quotations and allusions; historical and biblical references; motto beginnings and verse endings

10

(often original); negatives and "un words"; superlatives; dramatic, imaginative phrases; and alliterative, rhythmic lines.

Latinisms

In scholarly or literary prose, one expects an overuse of Latinisms, if only to exhibit a skill; but it seems peculiarly out of place in the rough-and-tumble of the early American political disputes. Yet there we find Freneau trying to hold his own, in a style branding himself as the author.

In the National Gazette editorials we see him using insular for island (adjective), requisites for needs, effusion for shedding, meliorate for improve, chimerical for impractical, ebullitions for products, eulogium for praise, exalted for high, communicate for impart, excursion for trip, appellation for name, etc.

In the NG essays probably his, we see the same habit--quondam for former, countenance (verb) for favor, veneration for respect, effervescence for expression, execrate for condemn, divine for know, importunate for urgent, elucidate for explain, etc.

His sentences reflect a literary background--balanced and parallel structure, or the reversed verb-subject order. He would often throw in, without warning, nautical terms, even with latitude and longitude, or verse, borrowed or original. On human and personal issues, he tended to become incoherent; when calm, his view was historical and philosophical. Frequently he used I or me--Hamilton never did so.

11

Favorite Words and Phrases

Freneau used terms like O, ye, and alas frequently, and the biblical or Quaker thee, thou, thy, hath, and -eth verbs. Some of his words almost never appeared elsewhere in newspapers--abode, animadversions, arrant, avow-avowed (adjective), base (adjective), be (subjunctive), but (only), calumny-calumniate-calumnious, dear (expensive), dismal, deem, eagle-eyed, generality (majority), gentry, had (if), thrice happy, ill (adverb), in vain or invain, lucubrations, luminary (sun), nay, mode, Machiavellian, paltry, parcel (of men), sanguine, servile, set or sett (of men), slavish, sycophant, trifling (small), very (adjective), vile-vilify-vilification, yoke, and zeal.

Favorite phrases were cacoethes scribendi, horrida bella, O tempora! O mores! shadow of merit, court-fed minions, masked duplicity, unblushing emissaries, fabric of wealth, loaves and fishes, yoke of foreign tyranny, atrocious insolence, friends of mankind, annals of history, one of the swinish multitude, God knows-God only knows-Heaven knows-Heaven only knows-Lord bless us-Lord deliver us- war-worn veteran, veil of secrecy, fruits of industry, set of blackguards, etc.

Actual Quotations

Retorting to NG attacks, Fenno evidently wrote this (GUS, July 11, 1792):

> Considering that the opposers of the measures...
> are generally the same persons who opposed the
> ...Constitution, and were the advocates of com-
> mittee systems and paper expedients in the days
> of our humiliation; the conjecture appears to be
> well founded...certain it is, that the strictures...
> in the NATIONAL GAZETTE are designed to sub-
> vert the present harmony, peace and happiness of

the Union.

Hamilton as "Scourge" (GUS, Sept. 22, 1792) thus attacked Jefferson:

> At Paris, Mr. J----, the representative of the American nation, wished for Union, because it would promote its prosperity, and enhance his dignity; but at Philadelphia, Mr. J---- fears in Mr. Hamilton a formidable rival, and therefore the sooner he can ruin in the public estimation, the better for his purpose. To this end were all his means to be directed--on the one hand, a monstrous affectation of pure republicanism, primitive simplicity, and extraordinary zeal for the public good--on the other hand, to cry down the funding system, the bank, the excise law, as emanations from the Secretary of the Treasury.

The noticeable characteristics of these Federalist essay styles are logic, common sense, clarity, calmness, and an absence of rhetoric and literary references.

A contrast is found in Republican writings. It was probably Edmund Randolph who as "Aristides" (GUS, Sept. 8, 1792) tried to answer Hamilton's attacks on Jefferson:

> In respect to the other charge of the advice given by Mr. Jefferson to the former Congress concerning the French debt, it is worthy to remark, that the accuser skulks from the charge... stabbing the reputation of an old meritorious public servent, by an unwarrantable conclusion, whilst he disavows a recollection of the facts.

This is somewhat more emotional than the Federalist essays. Freneau is even more lively and literary; apparently editorializing as "L.", he replied to Fed attacks (NG, Aug. 8, 1792):

> The melancholy howlings that have for some time past been heard through the dreary regions of the Gazette of the United States, are a full and clear proof that all is not right...

13

The devil rageth when his time is short...The
hackneyed cry of "the government is in danger"
has been too often repeated...

The funding system has had its day...it will be the
part of future legislatures...to develope the system
of iniquity that has robbed the soldier of his just
dues, and...has not spared to the orphan, the
widow, the halt or the blind, the helpless or the
infirm, the wretched pittance that opportunity pre-
sented a change of filching from their unsuspicious
hands.

James Monroe, defending Jefferson and Freneau from
Hamilton, wrote a series for ADA, reprinted in GUS; and he
thus retorted (GUS, Oct. 24, 1792):

The dispensation of the clerkship of foreign correspondence upon Mr. Freneau is the next circumstance...The appointment of this gentleman to
that situation has been deemed an act of such
enormity, that, like the original sin of our first
parents, it could never be expiated...

The compensation of 250 dollars per annum will
invite no respectable character from a distant
State to abandon a lucrative profession, or the
comfortable ease of private life. Nor will it in-
duce...any person to accept it...to whose ordinary
subsistence it would not yield a considerable aid.

But this is ponderous. For a change let us peruse
one of Freneau's short editorials (NG, Oct. 17, 1792):

The science of public paper, one would imagine,
ought to be rendered as simple as possible,
instead of being overshadowed with that studied
obscurity which more or less envelops the monied
concerns of almost every nation...There is no
science but may be made plain by laying down and
explaining the first principles; but by presenting
the complex fabric without clue or explanation,
the common enquirer is at once lost in a labyrinth
of uncertainty...Hence certain pecuniary advantages
are restricted to a few, and altho' a man may be
eagle-eyed in other matters, if he be not one of

14

those few, and admitted into the political holy of holies, he forever remains ignorant and blind to these mysterious affairs.--The dullest genius, however, when once initiated, is equal to the brightest; it is even a common observation that gravity succeeds best in such matters--

So have I seen from Schuylkill's brink
A flock of geese jump down together,
Swim, where the bird of Jove would sink,
And swimming, never wet a feather.

Freneau's lively style, or one probably his, was novel and distinctive among both Federalist and Republican political writings of his day. A casual reader would expect to find it only in belles lettres, so that, when seen in the brawling essays of politics, it is electrifying. His pieces act like beacons in the twilight of plodding debates and chaotic, angry accusations. Hamilton's are also quickly noticed; but he seldom used literary allusions or verse. Freneau's cry out, "I was written by Freneau!" No wonder the keen Hamilton said, referring to him, "Whenever the editor appears it is in correspondent dress."[11]

Punctuation

Freneau overused dashes, especially when indulging his Sternesque "Slender" manner. He asked many questions for dramatic effect. He inserted numerous exclamation marks, often in twos and threes (!!!), and italics liberally, for emphasis.

Alliteration

None of Freneau's writing habits, except the use of verse, is so typical of him--done almost unconsciously--and so uncharacteristic of other writers of the time, as his

15

alliteration--"lovers of liberty", "practices of princes", "clue of conspiracy", "sequestered solitudes", etc. This is the poet in prose. And who but a poet in a political essay, of all places, would write, "You are still under the influence of the magic of the scepter" or "prostrate the republican character at the shrine of Plutus?" Freneau was forever giving his prose the flavor of a poetic touch.

In two essay series far apart, The Pilgrim (1781-82) and the Slender Letters (1799-1801), one literary and "learned", the other political and "ignorant", we find similar styles. Like Hamilton, Freneau made little effort to conceal his natural manner, and--despite frequent shifts of pseudo-nyms--constantly revealed himself by his style.

The Method of Ascribing

In assigning "probables", it has been not one or two mannerisms, but several, along with ideas and circumstances, that determined the ascription. Very likely some errors have been made; but the great majority of these ascriptions will "probably" stand. Let us bear in mind that if Freneau had collected his prose as avidly as his poetry, we would have ample verification for most of these items. And their omission, merely for lack of 100% proof, would seriously affect the whole picture of the author's achievement, because most of these are closely related to known works.

It is both logical and proper to present probable works where the weight of evidence points to them. If style were the only criterion, wariness would be justified. But where style, content, and circumstances combine to point to the author, a refusal of a conditional ascription is carrying timidity too far. How could Freneau have foreseen that anyone would be so interested in his prose--particularly

16

the political essays--as to expect impregnable evidence of authorship? Most were dashed off to meet the next deadline, or to answer a rival's attack of yesterday, perhaps on the morning of his evening issue. He would be honored by our interest, but astonished. Let us consider his prose, and its many highly imaginative pseudonyms, in the light of the turbulent atmosphere in which it was born, out of a literary, emotional, creative mind.

Pseudonyms

From over 1100 items, over 300 pseudonyms emerge, listed under "certain" and "probable". Leary's list, with corrections, is added.

Certain

A. B.	Harpax
Adam Blackbeard	Hawser Trunnion
Adam Buckskin	Heraclitus
Alexander Dismal	Hermes
The Author of the Poems	Hezekiah Salem
first published in News-	Jacob Whissel
papers	K.
Catholicus	K. V.
Christopher Clodhopper	Lucullus
C. Clodhopper	M.
Mr. Clodhopper	Martial jun.
Civis	Martinus Scriblerius
E.	A Member of the Lower
Encore	House
F.	A Monarchist
A Free Press	N.
G.	Oh La!

Opay Mico

Orestes

P. F.

The Philosopher of the Forest

A Pilgrim

The Pilgrim

Plus Ultra

The President of the Debtor's
    Club

Priscilla Tripstreet

Pylades

R.

A Republican

Robert Slender

Simon Simple

Slender Thomas

Sylvius

Tomo Cheeki

The Translator

A Traveller

U.

Universal Justice

Virginius

W. H.

X

Z

♄ ♌ ♃   Saturn, Leo(?),
Jupiter

Probable

Abishag*****

Above-Board

Agricola

Alcanor

Alfred

An American

The American

American Sailor

Americanus

Americus

Anthero

Anti Candide

Anti-Puff

An Anxious Observer

Apuletus's Ass

Archimedes

Artist

Atticus

A. Z.

Barnaby Bodkin

Benedict Arnold

Bobby Tipstaff

A Bookseller

Brimborion

Broadbrim

A Brother Cit.

Brother Tory

A Brother Tory

Brutus

Bunker-Hill

A By Stander

Caius Gracchus

18

Camillus
Candid
Candidus
Candour
Cato
Caution
Centinel
Chares
Chrisioliphus
Circumbendibus
A Citizen
A Citizen of New Jersey
A Citizen of the United States
A Citizen of those Times
Cleopatra
Codrus
Columbus
Condorcet
Considerator
Consistency
A Continental Soldier
Cornelia
Corrector
A. Countryman
D. Doubtful
Decius
Defecator
A Democrat
The Democrat
Democritus
A Dictionarian
D. K.

Don Quixotte
Eliza
An Enemy to Deists
Expositor
Faley
A Farmer
A Federalist
Fellow Citizen
Fillip
Flood
A Foe to Despotism and
    Intolerance
A Foe to Dirty Fellows
A Foreigner?
F---- P----
Francis Foresight
A Freeman
A Friend to Consistency
A Friend to Genius and the
    Arts
A Friend to the Independent
    Gazetteer
A Friend to Peace and
    Mankind
A Friend to the Navy
A Friend to the Treaty
A Friend to the Truth
A Friend to two Branches of
    the Legislature
Fudge
Fun Done Over
Gag

19

Gates

G. G.

Gracchus

Grant's Hill

Hamlet

A Hater of Sycophants

Henrietta Lively

Herman

The High Priest

A Hint

Honestus

Hop, Skip, and Jump

Hornet

The Horse Doctor

Hotonthologus

An Independent Federal
  Elector

Interrogator

Janus

Jarzy Blue

Jersey Blue

A Jersey Farmer

A Jerseyman

Joe Bunker

Joe Bunker, Jun.

Joe Bunker, Junr.

Joel Bunker, Jun.

John Bull

Jonathan

Jonathan Bunker

Jonathan Robbins

Juba

L.

Lamech

A Lover of Fun

Lucian

Lucy Wrinkle

Lysander

Magnet

A Man of 1775

Maria Shrivel

Mat. Moonshine, jun.

Matthew Ward

Menippus

Mentor

Mercator

A Merchant and Soldier of '76

A Militia Man

Miss Baboon

Momus

Monitor

Montgomery

Mum

Mutius

Nathan

Nathan Cornstalk

A Native American

Nauticus

Nerva

A New-Jersey Forge-Man

No Federal Suwarraw

Obadiah

Observator

An Observer

Oh Times! Oh Manners!
An Old Almanac-Maker
Old Continental Currency
An Old Ecclesiastic
An Old Man
An Old Man of Chester
  County
An Old Rat Catcher
An Old Sailor
An Old Soldier
The Old Soldier
O. M.
One of the Gallery
One of the People
One of the Swinish Multitude
Order
P----
Paley
Paradox
Patrick
Paulus
Pauper
Pennsylvanius
Peter Pasquin
Peter Plagiary
Philadelphus
Philanthropos
Philocles
Philodemos
Philogenet
Philokalos
Philo-Republicanus

Philo Scriblerus
Plain Sense
Pluto
Polly Bunker
Polly Peevish
Polymnia
Publius
Puff
Pythagoras
A Quondam Friend
A Real Republican
Reason
A Refugee
Regiphilus
A Republican
Republicanus
Richard Frugal
Ringdumfunnidos
Robt. Buckskin
  Bob Buckskin
Robin Wiseacre
R. S.
S.
A Sailor's Friend
Sancho
Sangrado
Saratoga
Scaevola
Scevola
Scourge
Secundum Quid
Semper Eadem

Semper Idem

Seventy Six

Several of the Militia of
   Morris County

Shamokin

Sharpshins

Sid Hamet Benengeli

Simon

Simon Steady

A Soldier

Somnus

A Spectator

Spintext

The Spirit of MDCCLXXVI

A Staunch Federalist

A Staunch Quid

Stench Coaxe

Stephen Strapandscrape

Stophel Funk

A Supporter of Royalty

Susanna Grizzle

T.

Tabitha Toothless

Taphna

Telescope

Tell

Tertium Quid

Thespis

Thomas Doubtful

Thomas Traffic

Timon

Timothy Deep

Timothy Meanwell

Timothy Tinker

Timothy Tremulous

Timothy Turnpenny

Tisiphone

Tobias Tamehair

Tom Grumbler

Tom of the Tap Room

Truth

Turgot

Veritas

Verus

Virginius Americanus

Vivat Rex et Regina

The Voice of the People

W----

W.

Warren

Watch

A Watchman

The Watchman

William Tell

W. T.

X. Y.

X. Y. Z.

Yorick

Your Conductitious

Zenas

Leary's List--Prose and Poetry[12]

A.	Myrtilla
A. B.	N.
Adam Bluebeard	N. R.
Cassibilan	Orestes
Catholicus	Philomeides
Christopher Clodhopper	The Pilgrim
Alexander Dismal	Plus Ultra
Dobbins	Priscilla Tripstreet
E.	Pylades
F.	R.
A Foe to Malice	R. R.
G.	Rusticus
G. C.	Serjeant Major
Harpax	Simon Simple
Hawser Trunnion	Sinbat the Sailor
Heraclitus	Sylvius
Hermes	T. B.
Justitia Fiat	Tantalus
K.	Timothy Taurus
K. V.	Tory
Lucullus	U.
M.	Virginius
Martinus Scriblerus	W. H.
A Monarchist	W. S.

ADA   The American Daily Advertiser, John Dunlap, editor-
publisher, Philadelphia. No. 508.

Aurora The General Advertiser, and Political, Commercial,
Agricultural and Literary Journal, Benjamin
Franklin Bache, editor-publisher to 1798; William
Duane thereafter except a year or so, 1813-1815--
Philadelphia. "Aurora" was in title's center and
usurped the name. Nos. 424, 426, 427, 439,
440, 465, 469, 473, 499, 507, 515, 528, 565-
568, 570, 571, 588-609, 613, 616, 625, 640,
645, 660, 667, 671, 673, 674, 681-688, 777,
781, 810, 813, 816, 817, 820-823, 825-883, 887-
904, 909, 910, 912-914, 916-921, 925-929, 934-
1070, 1072-1081, 1083-1118, 1120, 1122, 1123,
1125-1133, 1143-1145.

BAL   Bibliography of American Literature, by Jacob N.
Blanck, New Haven, 1955-59, in process. Vol.
III, on Freneau, pages 244-256.

CG   The City Gazette, John Markland and John M'Iver,
publishers, Charleston, S. C. Nos. 134-138, 900.

CH   The Columbian Herald, Thomas Bowen and John
Markland, publishers, Charleston, S. C. No. 122.

DA   The Daily Advertiser, Francis Childs and John
Swaine, publishers, Childs the responsible editor;
Freneau "assistant editor", March 1790, to
March (?), 1791--New York. Nos. 187, 192-259,
261-279.

The Fredonian, D. and J. Fitz Randolph, publishers, New
  Brunswick, N. J. No. 1071

FJ The Freeman's Journal, Francis Bailey, editor-
   publisher, Philadelphia. Nos. 9-124, 126-131,
   188, 190, 191, 280. Freneau acted as "assistant
   editor" Aug. , 1781, to Sept. , 1782.

GSG Gazette of the State of Georgia, James Johnston,
   publisher, Savannah. No. 189.

GUS Gazette of the United States, John Fenno, editor-
   publisher; John Ward Fenno, from 1798-1800(?)--
   Philadelphia. Nos. 304, 365, 367, 371.

JC Jersey Chronicle, Philip Freneau, editor-publisher-
   printer, Middletown-Point, N. J. Nos. 610-612,
   614, 615, 617-624, 626-634, 641-644, 646-659,
   661-666, 668-670, 672, 675-679.

Leary Lewis Leary, That Rascal Freneau, New Brunswick,
   N. J. , 1941, with prose-poem bibliography. His
   Last Poems of Philip Freneau, New Brunswick,
   1945, adds more poems.

MA The Monmouth Almanac (for 1795), by Philip Freneau,
   Middletown-Point, N. J. , 1794. Nos. 572-587.

MHA Monmouth Historical Association, Freehold, N. J.

MW The Miscellaneous Works of Mr. Philip Freneau,
   Philadelphia, 1788. Nos. 139-185.

NG National Gazette, Philip Freneau, editor; Childs and
   Swaine of DA, publishers, Philadelphia. Nos.
   281-303, 305-364, 366, 368-370, 372-423, 425,
   428-438, 441-464, 466-468, 470-472, 474-498,
   500-506, 508-514, 516-527, 530-564.

NJG New-Jersey Gazette, Isaac Collins, editor-publisher,
   Trenton. No. 8.

NYA The Argus, called "The New-York Argus", Thomas
     Greenleaf, editor-publisher, New York. Nos.
     680, 818.

NYJ The New-York Journal, Thomas Greenleaf, editor-
     publisher, New York. Nos. 811, 814.

Paltsits A Bibliography of the Separate and Collected Works
     of Philip Freneau, by Victor H. Paltsits, New
     York, 1903.

Poems 1786 Poems: The Poems of Philip Freneau,
     Philadelphia, 1786.

     1795 Poems: Poems written between the years 1768
     & 1794, Mount-Pleasant, N. J., 1795.

     1809 Poems: Poems written and published during the
     American Revolutionary War, Philadelphia, 1809.
     2 vols.

     1815 Poems: A Collection of Poems...written be-
     tween the year 1797 and the Present Time, New
     York, 1815.

TA   The True American, James Wilson, editor-publisher,
     Trenton, N. J. Nos. 905-908, 911, 915, 922-924,
     930-933, 1134-1142.

TP   The Time Piece, Philip Freneau, editor, co-pub-
     lisher with Alexander Menut and Matthew Davis,
     New York. Nos. 689-776, 778-780, 782-809,
     812, 815, 818, 824.

USM United States Magazine, Hugh Brackenridge, editor--
     published by Francis Bailey--Philadelphia. Nos.
     2-5.

WM   The New-York Weekly Museum, James Oram,
     editor-publisher, New York. Nos. 1082, 1121,
     1124.

1   The Prose of Philip Freneau, Philip M. Marsh, editor,
    New Brunswick, N. J., 1955. This is the only col-
    lection of the prose since 1799.

2   Fred L. Pattee, "Bibliography of Philip Freneau",
    The Bibliographer, March 1902--poems only. Pattee
    edited The Poems of Philip Freneau, Princeton,
    1902-1907, three volumes. In Volume III, he in-
    cluded a partial list of the poems. His "Life of
    Philip Freneau," I, xiii-cxii, was long rated the best
    Freneau life. The whole work will be referred to as
    Pattee.

3   Victor H. Paltsits, A Bibliography of the Separate and
    Collected Works of Philip Freneau, New York, 1903.
    Hereinafter called Paltsits.

4   Lewis Leary, That Rascal Freneau, New Brunswick,
    1941, biography with long bibliography of prose and
    poetry. Hereinafter referred to as Leary. Leary
    edited The Last Poems of Philip Freneau, New
    Brunswick, 1945, which adds more poems and pseudo-
    nyms.

5   Jacob N. Blanck, Bibliography of American Literature,
    New Haven, 1955-1959, 3 vols., in process. Vol.
    III, 244-256 on Freneau, deals mostly with poems.
    Hereinafter called BAL.

6   The Miscellaneous Works of Mr. Philip Freneau,
    Philadelphia, 1788; and Letters...by Robert Slender,
    Philadelphia, 1799. Apparently only Freneau used
    the pseudonym "Robert Slender", which also appears
    in MW.

7   At the New Jersey Historical Society. The notes are in
    Freneau's hand, according to Paltsits; he put a
    "hook" on his preferred selections, evidently for
    publication in MW. See P. M. Marsh, "Philip
    Freneau's Personal File of "The Freeman's Journal",
    N. J. Historical Society Proceedings, April, 1939.

8   Leary, page 406; Last Poems, page xi.

9   The "Slender Thomas" letter (Aurora, Aug. 6, 1799)
    was excluded from the Slender Letters, but is ob-

viously part of the group, and is included here.
Freneau varied the Slender pseudonym by "A
Monarchist" and "Simon Simple", whose essays appear
in the Letters.

10   Within the Slender Letters, Freneau would doff the
      "Sternesque" manner, then resume it, as the whim
      moved him, or when his neighbor, the "Latinist",
      spoke.

11   Letter to Edward Carrington, May 26, 1792.

12   Leary, page 418. In remarks, Leary mentions "Robert
      Slender", "Hezekiah Salem", and "Sinbat". Though
      not signatures, "Tomo Cheeki" and "Opay Mico" are
      recognized by Leary. "Adam Bluebeard" should be
      "Adam Blackbeard" (MW, page 59). Omissions are
      the signatures of two Pilgrim essays, "X". (FJ,
      July 3, 1782) and "h.r.4." (FJ, July 24, 1782);
      "Dunmore" (1786 Poems, page 241); "James Riving-
      ton" (ibid., page 250); "Hugh Gaine" (ibid., page
      328); "P. F." (MW, page 403); "A News Printer"
      (1795 Poems, page 449); "Philip F----" (American
      Independence, 1778); "Don Quevado" (FJ, July 31,
      1782); and "Martial Jun". (Aurora, July 6, 1799),
      all with poems except the Pilgrim essays. Leary
      ignored "Jacob Whissel" (FJ, Aug. 7, 1782), though
      marked as his by Freneau in his personal file. In
      The Last Poems of Philip Freneau, Leary added
      "P. F.", "R", and "U".

Freneau's Published Prose

The list contains "certain" and "probable" ascriptions--
the first unmarked, the second marked with an asterisk (*).

1770

"Mr. Bombo's Pilgrimage to Mecca", short novel writ with
Brackenridge at Princeton in 1770. Ms. in William Brad-
ford's hand, in notebook at Historical Society of Penn-
sylvania. Freneau's part published by Lewis Leary as
"Father Bombo's Pilgrimage", Pennsylvania Magazine,
Oct., 1942, q. v.   1.

1779

United States Magazine, Hugh H. Brackenridge, editor,
Philadelphia. USM.
"Account of some of the West-India Islands, by a young
American Philosopher and Bel Esprit, just returned
from several small Voyages amongst those Islands.
Account of the Island of Bermuda, in a Letter to R. H.
Esq. (Extract)." Dated "Bermuda, May 10, 1778." USA,
Jan., 1779. Leary.   2.

"Account of the Island of Santa Cruz: Containing an Original
Poem on the Beauties of that Island." USM, Feb., 1779.
Leary.   3.

"Account of the Island of St. James," USM, March, 1779.
Leary.   4.

"Extract of a Letter containing an Account of a Cave, and a
Monument found in it"--USM, June, 1779. Elaboration,
with poem signed "F.", in TA, July 13, 1822.   5.

1780

"Some Account of the Capture of the Ship Aurora", ms. in
Freneau's hand at Rutgers University Library, evidently
writ in summer of 1780. Published in New York, 1899,
edited by Jay Milles--q. v.   6.

The Spy, incomplete play of three acts, a third in prose,
on Arnold and André, evidently writ in fall, 1780. Ms.
at Rutgers University Library.   In Pattee, Poems of
Philip Freneau, q. v. -1902.   7.

The New-Jersey Gazette, Isaac Collins, editor-publisher,
Trenton.
"To Sir Henry Clinton", rebuke for treatment of André--
NJG, Oct. 18, 1780. By "Z.", Freneau pseudonym--
see his poem "Reflections on the General Debased Con-
dition of Mankind," TP, Sept. 25, 1797, in the 1809
Poems as "On False Systems of Government," much
changed.   8.

1781

The Freeman's Journal, Francis Bailey, editor-publisher,
Philadelphia. Freneau was "assistant editor" Aug., 1781,
to Sept., 1782. Paltsits. FJ.

("Graduation Oratory on British Tyranny"), FJ, July 11, 1781.
By "Z.", Freneau pseudonym.   9.

("English Stubbornness"), editorial, FJ, Aug. 21, 1781.
Marked by Freneau in his personal FJ file.   10.

("British Troubles Abroad"), translated letter from Hispaniola,
FJ, Aug. 21, 1781.   11.

"The arcana of hell's politics"--Beelzebub surrenders Hell to
the British--FJ, Oct. 17, 1781.   *12.

("The Briton's Resemblance to Old-Mexican Indians"), editorial, FJ, Oct. 17, 1781.   13.

"A Dialogue between the United States of America and the
different Princes of Europe"--princes offer to be king of
America, but the United States declines the honor--FJ,
Oct. 24, 1781.   *14.

("Deane Refuted"), reply to Silas Deane's letters in Royal
Gazette--marked by Freneau as his in his file--FJ, Nov.
14, 1781. By "A Republican." (See also FJ, Dec. 5,
1781.)   15.

The Pilgrim series; FJ, Nov. 21, 28, Dec. 5, 12, 19, 26,
1781; Jan. 2, 9, 16, 23, 30, Feb. 13, 20, May 8, 29,
June 19, July 3, 24, Aug. 14, 1782. By "The Pilgrim."
Leary.

"The Pilgrim, No. I", on biography and ideals of supposed
author--FJ, Nov. 21, 1781. Signed "The Pilgrim," dated

"New Jersey, Nov. 16, 1781." In MW as "Philosopher of
the Forest," No. I. Leary.   16.

"The Pilgrim, No. II," on English eccentricities--FJ, Nov.
28, 1781. In MW as "Sentiments of a Traveller" and
"Philosopher of the Forest" No. V. Leary.   17.

("Deane Refuted," continued), FJ, Dec. 5, 1781. By "K.",
Freneau pseudonym.   18.

"The Pilgrim, No. III," on a rural parson and rural life--
FJ, Dec. 5, 1781. In MW as "Philosopher of the Forest,"
No. IV. Leary.   19.

("Americans are not English"), editorial, FJ, Dec. 12,
1781.   20.

"The Pilgrim, No. IV," on the parson, continued--FJ, Dec.
12, 1781. In MW as "Philosopher of the Forest," No.
VI. Leary.   21.

"The Pilgrim, No. V", more on English oddities--FJ, Dec.
19, 1781. Leary.   22.

("Definitions from The Royal Scotch Political Dictionary"),
satire on royalty and aristocracy--FJ, Dec. 19, 1781.
By "A Dictionarian."   *23

"The Pilgrim, No. VI," on benefits of solitude, the problem
of death and sleep, the folly of war--FJ, Dec. 26, 1781.
Leary.   24.

32

"The Pilgrim, No. VII"--the folly of duelling--FJ, Jan. 2,
1782. Leary. 25.

"The Pilgrim, No. VIII", on America's greatness--FJ, Jan.
9, 1782. In MW as "Philosopher of the Forest" No. X.
Leary. 26.

"The Pilgrim, No. IX", on servants, the stage, American
indifference to books--FJ, Jan. 16, 1782. Leary. 27.

("Let England Suffer Full Defeat"), editorial, FJ, Jan. 23,
1782. 28.

"The Pilgrim, No. X, " on Whigs and Tories--FJ, Jan. 23,
1782. In MW as "A Discourse upon Whigs and Tories."
Leary. 29.

("The New York Theater")--sarcasms on Rivington and Odell--
editorial, FJ, Jan. 23, 1782. 30.

"The Pilgrim, No. XI"--inadequacies of formal education,
preachers' use of Greek and Latin--FJ, Jan. 30, 1782.
Leary. 31.

"The Pilgrim, No. XII, " formal education and advantages of
rural life--FJ, Feb. 13, 1782. Leary. 32.

"The Pilgrim, No. XIII, " on Philadelphia political disputes--
FJ, Feb. 20, 1782. Leary. 33.

("Rebuke to 'F. H.'"), probably to Francis Hopkinson, for
   tolerating a Tory--FJ, March 6, 1782.   By "X. Y. Z." *34.

("'Calumniator's' Wish to be a Press Licenser"), attack on
   Hopkinson, apparently--FJ, April 10, 1782.   By "A Hater
   of Sycophants."   *35.

("Climate's Influence and Our Need of a Navy")--marked by
   Freneau as his, in his file--FJ, April 17, 1782.   (A
   small part is in MW as "Reflections, Narratives, and
   Ideas of the Late Robert Slender.")   Leary.   36.

("The Need of a Navy")--marked by Freneau as his in his
   file--FJ, April 24, 1782.   By "Orestes." Leary.   37.

("My Offer to Compromise"), evident satire on Hopkinson--
   FJ, April 24, 1782.   By "The High Priest."   *38.

"The Pilgrim, No. 14," on display of feminine charms,
   vanities of beaus, fashions--FJ, May 8, 1782. Leary. 39.

(Subsistence Rations for Army Officers")--FJ, May 15, 1782.
   By "Watch."   *40.

("British Plans to Subjugate America")--FJ, May 22, 1782.
   By "K.", Freneau pseudonym.   41.

"The Pilgrim, No. 15"--on Tories and "Tory words"--FJ,
   May 29, 1782.   Leary.   42.

"The Pilgrim, No. 16", on war's irrationality--FJ, June 19,
   1782. In MW as "Philosopher of the Forest"No. XI. Leary.
                                                          43.

("English Credulity"), marked by Freneau as his, in his
file--FJ, June 26, 1782. By "Hermes." Leary. 44.

"A Dialogue of the Dead," fictional talk between Dr. Warren
and Pitt--FJ, July 3, 1782. Marked by Freneau as his.
By "K. V." Leary. 45.

"The Pilgrim, No. 17," on lawsuits and lawyers--FJ, July
3, 1782. By "X." In MW as "A Discourse upon Law."
Leary. 46.

("Women's Fashions"), a criticism--FJ, July 10, 1782. By
"Christopher Clodhopper." In MW as "Interesting Thoughts,
Designed for the Public Good." Leary. 47.

("A Defense of Fashions")--FJ, July 17, 1782. By "Priscilla
Tripstreet." In MW as "Priscilla Tripstreet's Answer to
Christopher Clodhopper." Leary. 48.

("Retort to Miss Tripstreet")--FJ, July 24, 1782. By "C.
Clodhopper." In MW as "A Short Reply to the Above."
Leary. 49.

"The Pilgrim, No. XVIII," on city people's pettiness--FJ,
July 24, 1782. Signed ♄ ♌ ♃"(Saturn, Leo, Jupiter).
Leary. 50.

("A Defense of American Soldiers")--FJ, Aug. 7, 1782. By
"Virginius," Freneau pseudonym. 51.

("The Vile Ruffageze"), illiterate protest vs. Tories--FJ,
Aug. 7, 1782. By "Jacob Whissel." Marked by Freneau as his.
53.

"The Pilgrim, No. XIX," on cruelty to animals--FJ, Aug. 14, 1782. Leary. 54.

"A Short Catechism," satire on tax grumblers, marked by Freneau as his--FJ, Aug. 14, 1782. In MW as "A Political Catechism for Those whom it may Suit." Leary. 55.

("A Defense of Whigs and American Soldiers")--FJ, Aug. 21, 1782. By "Virginius," Freneau pseudonym. 56.

("Queries to Honest Jack"), sneers at John Dickinson--FJ, August 28, 1782. By "A Foe to Dirty Fellows." *57.

("Ship the Tories Away"), marked by Freneau as his--FJ, Aug. 28, 1782. By "Hawser Trunnion." Leary. 58.

"A Midnight Soliloquy in the Market House of Philadelphia"-- FJ, Sept. 4, 1782. By "W. H." Marked by Freneau as his. Leary. 59.

"A short account of the Bermuda or Summer islands, and some hints for reducing them to the obedience of the United States"--FJ, Sept. 4, 1782. By Harpax." Marked by Freneau as his. Leary. 60.

("Criticism of Salvation for All Men"), marked by Freneau as his--FJ, Sept. 11, 1782. By "A. B.", Freneau pseudonym. Leary. 61.

("Retort to Honest Jack")--FJ, Sept. 18, 1782. By "A Foe to Dirty Fellows." *62.

("Advice to The Independent Gazetteer"), satire--FJ, Sept. 18, 1782. By "A Friend to the Independent Gazetteer." *63.

("Farewell to Oswald"), in "Robert Slender" style--FJ, Sept. 25, 1782. By "A Friend to the Independent Gazetteer." *64.

("Lady in Greece to Lady in Paris"), translated letter from Mercury of France, marked by Freneau in his file--FJ, Oct. 9, 1782. *65.

The Dream of Momus series, satire on state assembly and Irish orators--FJ, Nov. 13, 27, 1782; Feb. 19, 1783. By "Momus." *

"The Dream of Momus," I--FJ, Nov. 13, 1782. By "Momus." *66.

"Intelligence Extraordinary," satire on Oswald, Dr. Rush, and his brother Jacob in editorial tone--FJ, Nov. 13, 1782. *67.

("An American Edition of the Bible"), praise for edition printed by Robert Aitken--FJ, Nov. 20, 1782. By "Catholicus" and marked by Freneau as his. Leary. 68.

("A Writer's Problems"), marked by Freneau as his--FJ, Nov. 20, 1782. By "Martinus Scriblerius." Leary. 69.

("False Dignity"), satire on "great" men, marked by Freneau as his--FJ, Nov. 20, 1782. By "G." In MW as "A Discourse on Esquires." Leary. 70.

"The Dream of Momus," II--FJ, Nov. 27, 1782. *71.

("Reply to 'A Friend to Mankind'"), more criticism of
Salvation for All Men, which "A Friend" defends in same
issue--FJ, Nov. 27, 1782. By "A. B.", Freneau pseudonym. (See FJ, Sept. 11, 1782.) 72.

("The Power of Oratory"), marked by Freneau as his--FJ,
Dec. 4, 1782. 73.

("On City Burying Places")--FJ, Dec. 11, 1782. In MW by
this title. By "R." Leary. 74.

("The Folly of Nicknames"), marked by Freneau as his--FJ,
Dec. 11, 1782. By "Plus Ultra." Leary. 75.

"To Mr. Waterposset," vulgar retort, apparently, to Jacob
Rush, with defense of Joseph Reed--FJ, Dec. 18, 1782. By
"A Quondam Friend." *76.

1783

("On Using the Sabbath"), marked by Freneau as his--criti-
cism of driving and barbering on Sunday--FJ, Jan. 8, 1783.
By "Heraclitus." Leary. 77.

"The Dream of Momus," conclusion--FJ, Feb. 19, 1783. *78.

"A few Reflections on reading the King's most gracious Speech
to his Parliament, on the 5th of Dec. 1782," criticism,
marked by Freneau as his--FJ, March 5, 1783. By
"Lucullus." Leary. 79.

"Sketch on Republics", translated from a "late French author,"
marked by Freneau as his--FJ, March 12, 26, 1783. By
"A. B." 80.

"Strictures on the Poem of Paradise Lost," translation from
the French Mercury of Jan., 1779--FJ, April 9, 1783--
marked by Freneau as his.   81.

"A Letter from St. Patrick to St. George," on life after
death--FJ, April 16, 1783. By "Patrick."   *82.

("The City's Silence on Peace News")--FJ, May 7, 1783.
By "Momus."   *83.

New Travels Through North-America, by Claude C. Robin,
translated by Philip Freneau, Philadelphia, 1783, from
Nouveau Voyage dans l'Amerique Septentrionale, Paris,
1782.   Thirteen letters written in 1781, at camps and
cities in the United States. Introduction, signed "The
Translator," and three footnotes by Freneau. (In TP,
March 15, 1797, Freneau says he translated the book.)
Advertised in FJ from July 30, 1783 (Leary, page 433).
BAL, Leary, Paltsits.   84.

"Introduction" of Robin's Travels, as above, by "The Translator."   85.

("British Debt Collectors")--FJ, Oct. 1, 1783. By "Americanus."   *86.

"Sleep!"--address to Sleep, like a prose "Night Thoughts"--
with, apparently, original verse. FJ, Oct. 15, 1783.   *87.

1784

("Origin of Despotism"), translated from Boulanger, with translator's comments--FJ, Jan. 7, 1784. Marked by Freneau as his.
                                                             88.

("Laws and Lawyers"), criticism in "Robert Slender" style--
FJ, Feb. 4, 1784. By "Robin Wiseacre." *89.

("Opposition to the Stage")--condemns glorifying royalty and
sneering at commoners on stage--FJ, Feb. 11, 1784.
By "Janus." *90.

("A Defense of the Stage")--FJ, Feb. 18, 1784. By
"Thespis." *91.

"The Restoration; or the Theatre Triumphant", comic play
on monarchy and current arguments over the theatre--
FJ, Feb. 25, 1784. *92.

("Answer to Thespis")--FJ, March 3, 1784. By Janus". *93.

("The Problem of Vice")--FJ, March 3, 1784. By "The
Watchman." *94.

"To Dr. Froth," probably to Benjamin Rush--taunts for
giving up attacks on state constitution--FJ, March 10,
1784. By "Publius." *95.

"To Philo Thespis and Janus", with quote from Sterne--FJ
March 10, 1784. By "Thespis." *96.

("The Plot against Press Freedom")--FJ, March 17, 1784.
By "Pennsylvanius." *97.

("A Wife's Complaint of her Husband")--in Sternesque style,
with Hamlet phrase, comic--FJ, March 24, 1784. By
"Abishag *****." *98.

("A 'Defense' of Canada"), mock praise, with note to Clay-
poole on how to run his paper--FJ, March 24, 1784.
By "Simon."   *99.

("Values of the Theater"), in "Slender" style, with quotes
from Sam Johnson and Congreve--FJ, March 24, 1784.
By "Thespis."   *100.

("Comments on the News"), in "Slender" style, with Addison
quote, comic--FJ, March 31, 1784. By "The Watchman."   *101.

("Literary Taste"), with Swift and Pope quotes--FJ, April
7, 1784. By "Reason."   *102.

("Defense of Blair's Lectures")--FJ, April 28, 1784. By
"Nerva."   *103.

("A Tribute to Sterne"), with original verse, "Alas! Poor
Yorick"--FJ, May 5, 1784. By "Nerva."   *104.

("No Mercy for Britons")--FJ, May 12, 1784. By "The
Watchman."   * 105.

("Our Dirty Streets"), support for Hopkinson's "Dialogue of
the Dead" (Pennsylvania Gazette, March 10, 1784)-- FJ,
June 23, 1784. By "Flood."   *106.

"Lucullus to the Western People", warning vs. British--FJ,
July 21, 1784. By "Lucullus," Freneau pseudonym--see
FJ, March 5, 1783.   107.

("Defense of the Episcopal Academy"), with Hudibras quote--
 FJ, Feb. 2, 1785. By "Candid."   *108.

"On the Volunteers of Ireland", criticism, with Shakespeare
 quotes--FJ, Feb. 2, 1785. By "An Old Man of Chester
 County."   *109.

("A Day with a Trimmer"), evidently satire on Dr. Rush--
 FJ, Feb. 9, 1785. By "A Traveller", Freneau pseudonym.
 (See "Sentiments of a Traveller," MW--and essay by "A
 Traveller," Sept. 20, 1797, whose character, Type, is
 same as in Freneau's poem, "The Country Printer,"
 1795 Poems, page 421.   110.

("The Sailor's Relief"), comic diary of sailor ashore--FJ,
 Feb. 16, 1785. In MW by this title. By "A.B."   111.

("An Assembly Speaker"), satire--FJ, Feb. 16, 1785. By
 "A Countryman."   *112.

("The Human Soul"), with Shakespeare quote--FJ, March 16,
 1785. In MW as "Robert Slender's Idea of the Human
 Soul." First description of the character later known as
 "Robert Slender."   113.

"Observations on the Discovery of the Philosopher's Stone,"
 FJ, March 23, 1785. By "T."   *114.

"Advertisement"--on futility of literary ambitions FJ, April 6,
 1785. By "A.B.", Freneau pseudonym.   115.

("Selling Books by Barter"), satire in "Slender" style--FJ,
   April 13, 1785. By "A Bookseller."   *116.

("Excessive Criminal Sentences"), with quote from Thomson's
   Seasons--FJ, July 13, 1785.   *117.

"Account of the annual Festivals of the Chinese, in honour of
   Agriculture," with Thomson quote--FJ, July 20, 1785. *118.

"A Dissertation on the Spartan State," with quote from Horace--
   FJ, Sept. 14, 1785.   *119.

"Description of a Fine Gentleman," satire--FJ, Sept. 21,
   1785.   *120.

"A Famous Axiom of Pope's defended"--on "Whatever is, is
   right", with criticism of Voltaire--FJ, Sept. 28, 1785.
   By "Anti Candide."   *121.

The Columbian Herald, Thomas Bowen and John Markland,
   publishers, Charleston, S. C.   CH.

"Petition from the Society of Old Maids, for a Tax upon the
   Old Batchelors"--CH, Oct. 3, 1785. Signed "Lucy
   Wrinkle," "Susanna Grizzle," "Maria Shrivel," "Polly
   Peevish," "Tabitha Toothless."   *122.

"On the Meanness and Malignity of Indolence," FJ, Oct. 5,
   1785.   *123.

"On Avarice," philosophical ridicule--FJ, Oct. 26,
   1785.   *124.

43

"A Short Account of the West Indies," including Freneau
poem, "These Indian Isles," Bailey's Pocket Almanac for
1787, Philadelphia, 1786. Poem in FJ, Jan. 31, 1787,
and the 1795 Poems. Here signed "K.", Freneau pseudonym. Leary.   125.

1787^2

("Labor-Saving Devices"), satire on inventions as a result
of laziness, with Virgil quote--FJ, Feb. 21, 1787.   *126.

("Stoves in Churches"), satire on stoves as conducive to
sleep, with Ovid quote--FJ, Feb. 21, 1787.   *127.

"Thoughts on Wishing," with quote from Young's "Night
Thoughts," satire--FJ, March 21, 1787.   *128.

"Serious Reflections--address'd to Hearts of Sensibility," like
Sterne--comic despair at western emigration's depopulation
of eastern cities--FJ, April 4, 1787. By "Your
Conductitious."   *129.

("Webster and his Title"), satire in "Slender" style on Noah
Webster's pride in esquire-- FJ, April 25, 1787. By
"Lamech."   *130.

"Reflections of a Pennsylvania Countryman," for proposed
federal constitution--FJ, Nov. 7, 1787. By
"Defecator".   *131.

"The Editor to the Reader," part of Preface to Freneau's
Journey from Philadelphia to New-York, comic poem by
"Robert Slender", Philadelphia, 1787. By
"Adam Buckskin."   132.

"Of the Nature of the Poem," in Preface of Journey, as in
No. 132. By "Adam Buckskin."   133.

1788

The City Gazette, John Markland and John M'Iver, publishers,
Charleston, S. C.

A Pilgrim series: CG, Feb. 4 (missing but referred to
Feb. 5), 5, 12, 16, 25, 1788. Titled "From a Cave,"
signed "A Pilgrim," a signature virtually identical with
"The Pilgrim" in FJ of 1781-82. Freneau was in
Charleston at the time--see Leary, pages 153, 383.

("Treat Debtors Liberally"), vs. enforced payment of mort-
gages, etc.--CG, Feb. 5, 1788, "continued from yesterday's paper." By "A Pilgrim."   134.

("A Ten-Year Payment of Debts"), appeal to legislature--CG,
Feb. 12, 1788. By "A Pilgrim."   135.

("Unjust Debt Laws"), CG, Feb. 16, 1788. By "A
Pilgrim."   136.

("Financial Calamity Coming"), CG, Feb. 25, 1788. By
"A Pilgrim."   137.

45

"On the Instability of Human Happiness," with Shakespeare
and Soloman quotes--FJ, March 19, 1788. By
"Sincerus." *138.

The Miscellaneous Works of Mr. Philip Freneau, Philadelphia,
1788. MW. Advertised in FJ, April 23, 1788, as
"Miscellanies." Contains first essay by "Robert Slender."
BAL, Leary, Paltsits.

By "Robert Slender"-

"Advice to Authors," MW, pages 42-48--with elaborate footnote description of "Robert Slender." 139.

"Robert Slender's Idea of the Human Soul," MW, pages
87-91. 140.

"An Oration upon Rum," MW, pages 91-92. 141.

"The Market Man," a character, MW, pages 93-94. 142.

"The Man in Business," a character, MW, pages 94-95. 143.

"The Man out of Business," a character, MW, pages
95-96. 144.

"The Debtor," a debtor's terror at creditors, MW, pages
96-97. 145.

"Rules and Directions, How to Avoid Creditors, Sheriffs,
Constables, &c."--MW, pages 97-106. 146.

"The Private Tutor," strong satire, MW, pages 106-111. 147.

"Light, Summer Reading," story, satire on love romances--
includes four poems--MW, pages 251-269.   160.

"Narratives, Observations and Advice on Different Subjects,"
MW, 269-281.   161.

"Reflections, Narratives, and Ideas of the late Robert Slender,"
in six parts, MW, pages 352-360.   162.

"A Discourse upon Whigs and Tories, by Mr. Slender",
satire on Tories and the Royal Gazette, MW, pages 367-
375. From "Pilgrim X," FJ, Jan. 23, 1782.   163.

Other, individual items in MW--

"The Picture Gallery," satire on fame-seeking, MW,
pages 49-53.   164.

"A Discourse upon Beards," on a club including Slender,
and including "A Lecture on Beards" by "Adam Black-
beard"--MW, pages 54-59.   165.

"The Antiquarian," satire on scholars, MW, pages
60-64.   166.

"The Sailor's Relief," comic plight of sailor ashore, MW,
pages 81-87. By "Alexander Dismal." From FJ essay,
Feb. 16, 1785, by "A. B."   167.

"Sentiments of a Traveller," on American prosperity, MW,
pages 311-313. From "Pilgrim II," Nov. 28, 1781.   168.

"The Philosopher of the Forest. Numb. II"--dream of
creation of man and beasts--MW, pages 290-298.   176.

"The Philosopher of the Forest. Numb. III"--continuation
and conclusion of No. 176--MW, pages 299-305.   177.

"The Philosopher of the Forest. Numb. IV", of a country
parson and rural life--MW, pages 305-311. From
"Pilgrim III," FJ, Dec. 5, 1781.   178.

"The Philosopher of the Forest. Numb. V"--on English
eccentricities--MW, pages 314-319. From FJ, Nov. 28,
1783.   179.

"The Philosopher of the Forest. Numb. VI"--concluding
story of parson in "Numb. IV"--MW, pages 320-325.
From "Pilgrim IV", FJ, Dec. 12, 1781.   180.

"The Philosopher of the Forest. Numb. VII"--tale of farmer
whose daughter-in-law upset his way of life--MW, pages
325-331. Satire on society, artificial life.   181.

"The Philosopher of the Forest. Numb. VIII"--dream essay
on the folly of fame and the brevity of life--MW, pages
332-343.   182.

"The Philosopher of the Forest. Numb. IX"--tale of Polish
peasant's hardships, the folly of expecting virtue--MW,
pages 343-351.   183.

"The Philosopher of the Forest. Numb. X"--on America's
greatness--MW, pages 360-367. From "Pilgrim VIII",
FJ, Jan. 9, 1782.   184.

"The Philosopher of the Forest. Numb. XI"--on war's
irrationality--MW, pages 375-380. From "Pilgrim XVI,"
FJ, June 19, 1782.   185.

"The Trial of Pleasure before the Judge Philosophy," tale
of victory of Pleasure, aided by Passions, over Philosophy
and Reflection--FJ, May 7, 1788.   186.

The Daily Advertiser, Francis Childs and John Swaine,
publishers--Childs evidently the responsible editor, Freneau
assistant editor March, 1790-March (?), 1791--New York.
Paltsits.   DA

"Extract of a letter from Capt. P. Freneau," on near wreck,
from Norfolk, dated July 29, 1788--DA, Aug. 13, 1788.   187.

Letter to Francis Bailey, on near wreck, from Norfolk,
dated Aug. 6, 1788--FJ, Aug. 20, 1788.   Leary.   188.

Gazette of the State of Georgia, James Johnston, publisher,
Savannah.

"Extract of a letter from Capt. Freneau, dated Norfolk, July
31, 1788," under Charleston news, so probably to Peter
Freneau--GSG, Aug. 28, 1788.   189.

("Wit and Beauty vs. Gold"), gay comment on love with quotes
from Hudibras and Volpone--FJ, Sept. 10, 1788.   By
"Chrisiophilus."   *190.

Letter to "A. B." (Andrew Brown?), who sent it to Bailey--
on sailor's stoicism, dated Savannah, March 14, 1789--
FJ, July 8, 1789.   191.

(Essay, humorous, on use of words, CG, Dec. 30, 1789-
Leary 384, Note 101.)

1790

("Odd Word Sources"), satire on Johnson's Dictionary--DA,
Feb. 18, 1790. By "M.", Freneau pseudonym (used with
Freneau poem, "Lines descriptive of a Tavern at Log-
Town," DA, Feb. 19, 1790.)   192.

"Some Account of the Manners and Condition of the Georgia
Negroes," in reply to certain articles for slavery--DA,
March 30, 1790. By "X. Y. "   *193.

"A brief account of the Ugly Club, held in one of the southern States, and their usual mode of procuring new Members"--DA, April 5, 1790. In MA. Leary.   194.

"Anecdotes, and Sketch of the Character, of Doctor Franklin"--
DA, April 24, 1790. Apparently an editorial filler.   195.

"Translation of a letter from a French gentleman, settled in
one of the United States, to his friend in one of the French
West India Islands, 1790"--propaganda for immigrants--
DA, May 5, 7, 1790. Sounds like Crevecoeur--may well
be a hoax.   *196.

("Militia Should Not be under Federal Control"), DA, May 7,
1790. By "A Militia Man."   *197.

52

"Description of New-York one hundred and fifty years hence,"
forecast of growth and improvement--DA,   June 12, 14,
1790.   By "A Citizen of those Times."   *198.

"Lady Bab's Soliloquy"--satire on cosmetics and red hair--
DA, June 17, 1790.   By "Miss Baboon."   *199.

"A Speech on a New Subject," on the retired sea captain
ashore--DA, June 29, 1790.   As "Tomo Cheeki XI,"
JC, August 15, 1795.   200.

"An Oration in commendation of Tobacco," DA, June 30,
1790.   Introduced by "A. B.", Freneau pseudonym--
with Shakespeare quote.   201.

"The Old Soldier and his Dog," story of the poor veteran--
DA, July 5, 1790.   *202.

("Shipping Duties and Laws"), protest vs. unjust regulations--
DA, July 5, 1790.   By "L."   * 203.

"Remarks on the Potowmac," for new location of government
as the best--DA, July 6, 1790.   By "Truth."   *204.

"Hint to the Public," on city's need of a park or art center--
DA, July 12, 1790.   Evidently an editorial.   205.

"Upon the Ancient Revolutions of Nature," translated from
Boulanger--DA, July 15, 1790.   206.

("Problem--a Home for Congress"), comic, nautical--DA,
July 15, 1790.   By "Hop, Skip and Jump."   * 207.

"On the advantages of Steadiness": mentions the Indian, Opay Mico, and is related to the "Tomo Cheeki" series--DA, Aug. 31, 1790. Leary. 217.

"A short discourse upon Drunkenness"--DA, Sept. 1, 1790. As "Tomo Cheeki IV," JC, June 20, 1795. By "Opay Mico." Leary. 218.

"Reflections on my Journey from the Tallassee towns to the settlements on the river Hudson"--"translated" from the "Tallassee language"--DA, Sept. 8, 1790. By "Opay Mico." Leary. 219.

"A Discourse upon Horse Shoes"--DA, Sept. 17, 1790. By "Opay Mico." As "Tomo Cheeki IX," JC, Aug. 1, 1795. Leary. 220.

("Reasons for Optimism in New York"), partly in "Slender" style--DA, Sept. 22, 1790. By "A Traveller," Freneau pseudonym. 221.

"Magistrates", editorial, that republican magistrates will be superior--DA, Sept. 29, 1790. 222.

"On Patriotism", editorial on world brotherhood, preferable to patriotism--DA, Sept. 30, 1790. 223.

("On Political Letters"), satire on Samuel Mitchill, doctor in politics, a congressman, now a candidate--DA, Oct. 14, 1790. By "Thomas Traffic." *224.

("Rules for a Young Printer"), comic advice--DA, Oct. 15,
1790. By "A. B.", Freneau pseudonym.   225.

"Of the Florida Gulph Stream," nautical description, editorial
filler--Oct. 16, 1790.   226.

"Thoughts on Masonry," editorial emphasizing masonry's
force for brotherhood--DA, Oct. 19, 1790.   227.

("Hints about the Balls"), light gossip--DA, Oct. 21, 1790.
By "Henrietta Lively."   *228.

("The Tennessee Country"), help for Morse, the geographer--
DA, Oct. 21, 1790. By "M.", Freneau pseudonym.   229.

"Letter to a newly elected Young Member of the Lower House",
satire on Congress and odd congressmen--DA, Oct. 22,
1790. By "A. B.", Freneau pseudonym.   230.

"A Discourse upon Barbers' Poles," farcical--DA, Nov. 1,
1790. In MA. Leary.   231.

"Pygmalion," translated from Rousseau, to be offered as
opera by "Mr. St. Aivre and Company" on Nov. 4--DA,
Nov. 2, 3, 1790.   232.

"On the national character of the Spaniards", translation from
Nouveau Voyage en Espagne, DA, Nov. 4, 1790.   233.

"On Propriety of Situation in public Buildings and public
Places", editorial--DA, Nov. 5, 1790.   234.

"Natural History," description of the White Mountains, editorial filler--DA, Nov. 6, 1790.   235.

("Despotism"), translated from Boulanger's Origine du Despotisme--DA, Nov. 6, 1790.   236.

"Description of the Falls of Niagara", editorial filler--DA, Nov. 8, 1790.   237.

"Description of a North-Carolina Ordinary, (or Inn)"-- evidently from first-hand experience--DA, Nov. 10, 1790.   *238.

"Rules how to compliment great Men in a proper manner", satire on poem overpraising Jefferson--DA, Nov. 11, 1790.   By "A. B.", Freneau pseudonym.   239.

"General Character of the Insular West India Creoles", editorial, DA, Nov. 12, 1790.   240.

"On the Liberty of the press in England," editorial--DA, Nov. 13, 1790.   241.

"A Georgia Planter's method of spending his time," editorial filler, apparently from personal observations--DA, Nov. 13, 1790.   242.

("The Derivation of Church"), editorial on essay in Connecticut paper--DA, Nov. 15, 1790.   243.

"On Epic Poetry", editorial satire on American epics, with an eye to those by the Connecticut wits--DA, Nov. 18, 1790   244.

("The Cruelty of Popery"), reply to defense of the Inquisition--
DA, Nov. 18, 1790. By "A Foe to Despotism and Intol-
erance."   *245.

("New York Can Support a Theater"), editorial--DA, Nov.
27, 1790.   246.

"On the power of Chance in the production of Great Charac-
ters", editorial referring to Vaucanson, Shakespeare,
Cromwell, Rousseau, Milton, Molière, and Corneille--
DA, Nov. 27, 1790.   247.

"On Funeral Elogiums", editorial satire of poems writ in
bad taste--DA, Dec. 8, 1790.   248.

("Connecticut Wonders"), sarcastic--DA, Dec. 11, 1790.
By "D. Doubtful."   *249.

("Defense of Connecticut"), ironic boasting of a seed produc-
ing 200 squashes, a 140-pound pumpkin, mothers of
triplets and quads, who would write more epics, etc.--
DA, Dec. 14, 1790.   *250.

"Reflections on Sundry subjects," editorial retort to slur on
"Volumes of scraps gathered together from old newspapers, under the title of poems," and to praise for
Connecticut epics (DA, Dec. 15); and defense of Freneau's
work--DA, Dec. 16, 1790.   251.

"To the Author of the Address, &c. in yesterday's paper",
editorial retort to writer who, in DA of Dec. 17, had
slurred "verses which the author compliments with the
58

'title of poems'". Here Freneau assumes his critic to be
a Tory--DA, Dec. 18, 1790. By "The Author of the
Poems first published in Newspapers." Leary   252.

"Parallel between France and England"--translation from
   French paper, favoring France--DA, Dec. 20, 1790. 253.

("Creditors are Happy with the Funding System"), veiled
   satire--DA, Dec. 27, 1790. By "Consistency."   *254.

1791

("Pennsylvania's Meddling with Congress"), editorial--DA,
   Jan. 27, 1791.   255.

("The Ward-Division Proposals"), comic talk on proposals to
   split city into wards--DA, Jan. 28, 1791. By "A Lover
   of Fun."   *256.

("Defense of Truth's Plan"), Sternesque style, nautical
   terms, on ward plan--DA, Feb. 3, 1791. By "Fun Done
   Over."   *257.

"Extract of a letter from London, Nov. 30"--tells of perform-
   ance on stage of Freneau's "law case between Solomon
   Dash and Frederick Flute," item in MW--Leary (page 386)
   found no evidence; it was hoax, probably--DA, Feb. 11,
   1791.   258.

"On Notions," editorial satire on odd ideas--DA, Feb. 11,
   1791.   258a.

   "Character of the Spanish Women,"editorial filler--DA, Feb.
   11, 1791.   259.

Proposals for a Monmouth Newspaper, New York, Feb. 15, 1791. Project never fulfilled. Leary, Paltsits. 260.

("Our Vendue System"), protest at possible monopoly, possible evasion of taxes--DA, Feb. 23, 1791. By "Candidus." *261.

("Bible Inconsistencies"), on reasons for differing accounts-- DA, March 5, 1791. By "Timothy Meanwell." *262.

("Free Elections' Benefits"), DA, April 21, 1791. By "Philokalos." *263.

("Keep the Trees"), editorial on same page, but separated from Freneau's poem, "The Landlord's Soliloquy," on same subject; listed by Leary as introduction to poem-- DA, May 31, 1791. By "Civis." Leary. 264.

("A Finee's Complaint"), on law fining sellers trading on city property--DA, June 15, 1791. By "Pauper." *265.

Philodemos series, for Paine's Rights of Man, vs. John Adams's Discourses on Davila--DA, June 21, 28, July 5, 26, Aug. 4, 12, 1791. By "Philodemos". *

("Self-Government and Liberty"), DA, June 21, 1791. By "Philodemos." *266.

("Men and Equality"), DA, June 28, 1791. By "Philodemos." *267.

Brutus series, reply to "Publicola" (John Q. Adams), defense of Paine and Jefferson--DA, June 28, 29, July 4, 6, 11, 15, 22, 1791. By "Brutus."   *

("Defense of Paine and Jefferson"), DA, June 28, 1791. By "Brutus."   *268.

("Publicola's Errors"), DA, June 29, 1791. By "Brutus."   *269.

("The Right to Change Laws"), DA, July 4, 1791. By "Brutus."   *270.

("The Folly of Balanced Powers and Monarchy"), DA, July 5, 1791. By "Philodemos."   *271.

("Publicola's False Assumptions"), DA, July 6, 1791. By "Brutus."   *272.

("Publicola's Falsities on the Rights of Man"), DA, July 11, 1791. By "Brutus."   *273.

"Translation. A letter from the Count de Mouslier to Mr. Necker"--on improving trade with America, dated New York, May 12, 1789--DA, July 12, 18, 1791.   274.

("French and English Constitutions and Legislatures"), DA, July 15, 1791. By "Brutus."   *275.

("Publicola's Masked Treachery"), DA, July 22, 1791. By "Brutus."   *276.

("Slavery in Europe and the West Indies"), editorial criticism

of London poem defending slavery--DA, July 23, 1791.
277.

("The Coming Democratic Revolution"), DA, July 26, 1791.
By "Philodemos." *278.

("Monarchy and Free Government"), DA, Aug. 4, 1791. By
"Philodemos." *279.

"Proposals for Publishing... The National Gazette... By
Philip Freneau"-- FJ, Aug. 24, Oct. 26, 1791. Also in
DA, Aug. 25-31, Sept. 1-5, 1791. Dated at Philadelphia,
Aug. 20, 1791. 280.

National Gazette, Philip Freneau, editor, published by Childs
and Swaine, Philadelphia, Paltsits. NG.

"To the Public," first editorial, on NG policies--NG, Oct.
31, 1791. Leary. 281.

("A Republic's Security from Usurpation"), translation from
a "late French Paper"--NG, Nov. 3, 1791. 282.

"To the Public," editorial on policies--NG, Nov. 7, 1791.
Signed "P. Freneau." 283.

"The interest of the Northern and Southern States forever
inseparable," editorial--NG, Nov. 10, 1791. 284.

("New England's Advantage in Reapportionment"), NG, Dec. 1,
1791. By "A. B.", Freneau pseudonym. 285.

"On the present state of Religion in Scotland," translated
   from "French letters, dedicated to the National Assembly"--
   on weakness of church in Scotland, decline of faith--NG,
   Dec. 8, 1791.   286.

"On the Pleasures of Ignorance," translated from "a late
   French Author"--NG, Dec. 15, 1791.   287.

1792

("Wallace and the Battle of Falkirk"), on presentation to the
   President of a box made from the Wallace Oak, gift from
   the Earl of Buchan--NG, Jan. 2, 1792.   Editorial.   288.

("Catholic Indulgences"), translation from Le Patriote Francois
   (see NG, Jan. 19, 1792), with "price current" for sins--
   NG, Jan. 12, 1792.   289.

("The Rights of an Indian"), dream essay, speech by ship's
   Indian head--NG, Jan. 12, 1792.   As "Tomo Cheeki VIII,"
   JC, July 25, 1795.   Leary, page 457.   290.

"Nobility," editorial on its absurdity--NG, Jan. 19,
   1792.   291.

("The Means to Ends"), editorial with original verse--NG,
   Jan. 19, 1792.   292.

"On Country Taverns," introducing Freneau poem, "The Jug
   of Rum"--NG, Jan. 23, 1792.   293.

("Catholic Indulgences Existed"), reply to "Zwinglius"
   (probably Mathew Carey) and "A Catholic"--NG, Jan. 23,

1792. By "Verus."   *294.

"Indian Antiquities," on supposed inscriptions by De Soto,
     editorial filler--NG, Feb. 6, 1792.   295.

"On the Origin of Nobility", editorial--NG, Feb. 6,
     1792.   296.

"Western Discoveries," editorial on explorations by Stuart,
     an Englishman--NG, Feb. 9, 1792.   297.

"Correspondence between Earl Cornwallis and Tippoo Saib,"
     editorial summary--NG, Feb. 20, 1792.   298.

"Hatteras Shoals," description with water depths, widths, etc.,
     an editorial filler--NG, March 8, 1792.   299.

("Members of Congress, Chief Gainers by New Laws"),
     defense of right to criticize public measures, from ADA,
     but in Freneau's style--NG, March 8, 1792. By "A
     Spectator."   *300.

"On Trees in Cities," introducing "The Landlord's Soliloquy,"
     Freneau poem (different essay from DA, May 31, 1791)--
     NG, March 8, 1792.   301.

"Mulattoes of St. Domingo," editorial filler--NG, March 12,
     1792.   302.

"A Description of the Dismal Swamp in Virginia," editorial
     filler--NG, March 12, 1792.   303.

Gazette of the United States, John Fenno, editor-publisher,
 Philadelphia. GUS.

("Applause in the House"), plea for applause--in NG, March
 19, 1792; same author in NG, May 10, 1792, with editor-
 ial--GUS, March 17, 1792. By "Encore. "   304.

("A Delaware-Susquehanna Canal"), editorial, NG, March
 19, 1792.   305.

"Remarkable Antiquities in interior America", editorial
 filler "From the manuscript of a late Traveller"--NG,
 March 22, 1792.   306.

"A modest Hint to the State Legislatures, " satire on closing
 Senate doors to public--NG, March 26, 1792. By "Above-
 Board. "   *307.

"Universal Peace, " for world government, paid for by
 2,000,000 acres annually rising from ocean--NG, April 2,
 1792. By "Magnet. "   *308.

("Representation of Free People Only"), on proposed act--
 NG, April 5, 1792. By "Plain Sense. "   *309.

("The New Tax, a Stamp?"), editorial warning vs. stamps
 and for hurry, as tax will help poor--NG, April 12,
 1792.   310.

("The Invalidation of Jackson's Election"), protest--NG,
 April 16, 1792. By "Anthero. "   *311.

NG, May 7, 1792. By "Archimedes." 321.

("Unjust Criticism in the Gazette of the United States"),
angry editorial retort to opposition to criticism of government, thinly disguised as a contribution--NG, May 10,
1792. By "Encore." 322.

("Certain Word Sources"), farcical explanation of sycophant,
gospel, bombazine, and aristocracy--NG, May 10, 1792.
By "Democritus." *323.

"To Sidney and the Whiskey-Drinkers", ironic defense of
excise, and satire of New England distillery congressmen--
NG, May 14, 1792. By "Mum." *324.

("The Evils of Usury"), editorial, recommending rate of 4%
--NG, May 14, 1792. 325.

"Of lake Superior, or, the upper lake", editorial filler--NG,
May 17, 1792. 326.

("Fenno's Puffing Editorial"), supporting "Encore" (NG, May
10)--NG, May 17, 1792. By "Anti-Puff," very like
"Encore." *327.

"Theatre", editorial for a republican stage, not one devoted
to heroism of tyrants--NG, May 21, 1792. 328.

"A new Grant to America!"--defense of right to freedom of
speech, protest at proposed restrictions of press, like an
editorial--NG, May 24, 1792. By "Corrector." *329.

achievement--NG, June 14, 1792.   340.

"Once More, Ye foreigners, attend!" --editorial retort to
    Fenno, defense of June 11 article by same author--NG,
    June 14, 1792. By "Oh, La!"   341.

"Excise Law," editorial protest--NG, June 18, 1792.   342.

"Manufactures", editorial suspicion of politics in new plans--
    NG, June 18, 1792.   343.

"Enemies to the Government!"--defense of foreigners and
    right to criticize government--NG, June 18, 1792. By
    "A Foreigner?"   *344.

("The Bank's Lending Method"), editorial criticism--NG,
    June 21, 1792.   345.

("The Cincinnati--the Evil in Titles"), quote from Annual
    Register for 1785, with comments--NG, June 21, 1792.
    By "W. T."   *346.

"New-York," introduction to Freneau poem, "The Demolition
    of Fort George," on city's better appearance--NG, June
    21, 1792. Poem in 1795 Poems. Leary, page 446.   347.

("Fenno's Vaporing Challenges"), editorial--NG, June 25,
    1792.   348.

"Remarkable Curiosity," on American mandrake's resemblance
    to human form, editorial--NG, June 25, 1792.   349.

69

"On the present state of the poor in England", editorial--
    NG, June 28, 1792.   350.

"Bank", vs. congressmen's participation, editorial--NG,
    July 4, 1792.   351.

("Fed Writers Profit by Issues they Defend"), suggestion of
    "vigilance societies"--NG, July 4, 1792. By "W.T."*352.

"Rules for changing a limited Republican Government into
    an unlimited hereditary one"-- like Franklin's "Rules"
    (1773), a sort of editorial--NG, July 4, 7, 1792.   353.

"A new sort of an Allegory", editorial on government com-
    pared to a ship--NG, July 7, 1792.   354.

("Enemies of the Constitution"), vs. monarchial politicians--
    NG, July 7, 1792. By "G.", Freneau pseudonym.   355.

"A Remarkable Circumstance of Escape", story of ship
    blown into Shrewsbury River and saved--editorial filler--
    NG, July 11, 1792.   356.

("Fed Claims in New York"), on New York election, refutation
    of Fed claims--"To the Printer," but in editor's style--
    NG, July 11, 1792.   357.

"Shrewsbury," intimate description, editorial filler--NG,
    July 14, 1792.   358.

("French Revolution, Sign of Universal Change"), editorial--
    NG, July 14, 1792.   359.

("The Feds Against the People"), editorial, NG, July 18,
1792.   360.

"Detached Thoughts on Elective Government," editorial on
evils of hereditary power in Europe--NG, July 18, 25,
1792.   361.

("Need of 'Constitutional Societies'"), editorial--NG, July
25, 1792.   362.

("Suppressing Public Opinion Dangerous")--NG, July 25,
1792. By "A Farmer."   *363.

("Reply to 'T. L.'")--Hamilton's accusation of Freneau as
editing under influence of his translating salary (GUS,
July 25) reprinted with editorial retort. Freneau thought
"T. L." was Fenno, at first. NG, July 28, 1792.   364.

("Freneau is a Free Editor"), with slap at Fenno, followed
by Fenno's denial of writing "T. L." attack--GUS, July
28, 1792. By "A. Z."   *365.

("Fed Fears"), like editorial, condemnation of funding system--
NG, Aug. 8, 1792. By "L."[3]   366.

"To the Public," Freneau's affidavit denying charges by "An
American" (Hamilton, GUS, Aug. 4), with other remarks--
GUS, Aug. 8, 1792. Signed "Philip Freneau, Editor of
the National Gazette."   367.

("The Federalist Money System"), condemnatory editorial,
NG, Aug. 11, 1792.   368.

("Ambitious Men, Dangerous in Republics"), probably writ
with an eye on Hamilton--NG, Aug. 11, 1792. By "A.
B. ", Freneau pseudonym.   369.

("Fenno's Treasury Income")--hints Fenno gets ten times
Freneau's salary, in printing work "exclusively" from
Treasury--NG, Aug. 15, 1792. By "G.", Freneau
pseudonym. But "Candor" (probably Hamilton, GUS,
Aug. 18) denied this, said Childs and Swaine got a large
share of the Treasury work.   370.

("Let 'An American' Support his Charges")--Freneau refuses
to answer anonymous attacks--GUS, Aug. 15, 1792.
By "The Editor of the National Gazette."   371.

To the People of the United States--two essays, first possibly
by Brackenridge, second probably by Freneau--defending
Republican ideas and criticizing Federalist positions--
NG, Aug. 15, 22, 1792. By "An Independent Federal
Elector."[4]   372.

("The Revolution in France"), editorial--NG, Aug. 18, 1792.
                                                            373.

("Hamilton's Obscure Reports, Dominance of the House"),
plea for simple reports--NG, Aug. 25, 1792. By
"Mercator."   *374.

("Wealth and Intelligence"), satire to chairman of Committee
of Correspondence, ironic idea that "understanding and
property are in direct ratio with each other", so that
only the wealthy should be elected--NG, Aug. 25, 1792.
By "Momus."   *375.

("On Cruelty to Animals"), editorial protest--NG, Aug. 29, 1792. 376.

("A Treasury Statement Error")--NG, Sept. 1, 1792. By "Mercator." *377.

"British Navy," editorial history--NG, Sept. 1, 1792. 378.

"Mercator to Civis," retort to "Civis" (NG, Sept. 5), who was Hamilton, suggesting Civis is Hamilton and should sign his name--NG, Sept. 8, 1792. By "Mercator." *379.

("Jefferson and his Accuser"), defense of Jefferson, criticism of Hamilton--NG, Sept. 8, 1792. Unsigned, to "Mr. Freneau." *380.

("McKean's 'Impartiality'"), satire on Thomas McKean, chairman of correspondence committee for candidates, in Sternesque style--NG, Sept. 19, 1792. By "Democritus." *381.

("Orthodoxy's Insistence on Conformity"), editorial with quote from Klimius' Subterranean Journey-- NG, Oct. 3, 1792. 382.

("Arbitrary Nominations"), for Congress nominations by the people--NG, Oct. 3, 1792. By "Z.", Freneau pseudonym. 383.

("Hamilton's Ideas on Public Debt"), criticism--NG, Oct. 10, 1792. By "Truth." *384.

("Double Motives in Politics"), veiled attack on Hamilton--
   NG, Oct. 13, 1792. By "Paradox."   *385.

("Obscurity in Money Matters"), editorial with verse--NG,
   October 17, 1792.   386.

("Public Debts are Not Blessings"), with quote from Pope's
   Moral Essays--NG, Oct. 17, 1792. By "Honestus." *387.

("Reply to Charges"), editorial--NG, Oct. 20, 1792. By
   "The Editor of the National Gazette."   388.

"Loves of the Plants," references to Linnaeus and Erasmus
   Darwin, with quote from Darwin poem--editorial filler--
   NG, Oct. 20, 1792.   389.

"'Facts Speak Louder than Words'"--criticism of government
   policies--NG, Oct. 20, 1792. By "Camillus."   *390.

("Defense of Indians"), editorial with verse--NG, Oct. 24,
   1792.   391.

("How to Lecture on Medicine"), satire with nautical terms--
   NG, Oct. 24, 1792. By "Peter Plagiary."   *392.

("Jefferson's Accuser is a Monarchist")[5]--NG, Oct. 24, 1792.
   By "Camillus."   *393.

"On the Indian War," editorial protest--NG, Oct. 27,
   1792.   394.

("The National Gazette's Policy"), editorial review--NG,

("Retort to Fact"), more on Fact's (Hamilton's) opinion on
the blessings of public debt--NG, Oct. 31, 1792. By
"Truth." *396.

"Detached reflections from a correspondent", on speculation,
mystery in government, profiteers, etc--despite title,
patently an editorial--NG, Nov. 3, 1792. 397.

("Federalist Evasions"), editorial--NG, Nov. 21, 1792. 398.

"Pro and Con, Arguments against the reëlection of Mr.
Adams", mostly on Adams's monarchism--NG, Nov. 24,
1792. By "Mutius." *399.

"Thoughts on Constitutions," translated from Condorcet--
NG, Dec. 5, 1792. 400.

"Cat-Island", editorial description, apparently from personal
observation, with Dryden verse from The Indian Emperour--
NG, Dec. 5, 1792. 401.

The Political Situation series: mostly editorial defense of
Clinton, candidate for Vice President--NG, Dec. 8, 12,
19, 1792; Jan. 12, 1793.

("Feds' Designs, Clinton, and Otsego's Attack"), editorial--
NG, Dec. 8, 1792. 402.

("Adams's Monarchism, Clinton's Republicanism"), editorial--
NG, Dec. 8, 1792. 403.

("A Confusion in Names"), defense of Clinton, editorial--NG,
Dec. 12, 1792.   404.

"A Suggestion," for a patent system financing inventors--NG,
Dec. 15, 1792. By "Artist."   *405.

("The Danger of Titles"), with quote from Pope--NG, Dec.
15, 1792. By "Condorcet."   *406.

"Sketch of the present situation of Vermont", editorial filler--
NG, Dec. 19, 1792.   407.

("Birthday Odes are Unrepublican"), probably aimed at plans
for celebrating Washington's birthday--NG, Dec. 19,
1792. By "G. G."   *408.

"A critical view of Parties in relation to the contest between
Mr. Adams and Governor Clinton," for Clinton--NG, Dec.
19, 1792. By "A. Z."   *409.

("Falsehoods about Clinton"), to "Otsego," editorial--NG,
Dec. 19, 1792.   410.

("Women's Influence in Politics"), vs. monarchism--NG,
Dec. 26, 1792. By "Cornelia."   *411.

("Power Belongs to People Only"), editorial--NG, Dec. 26,
1792.   412.

"A Great Fraud", tale of defrauded inventor, with appeal for
the Patent Bill--NG, Dec. 26, 1792. By "Artist." *413.

("American Republicanism and British Government"), editorial
--NG, Dec. 29, 1792. Criticism of Hamilton's management
of Congress, or "How to Relieve Congress from Thinking."
414.

1793

("The Kingly Party in America"), editorial--NG, Jan. 2,
1793.   415.

"A Statement of the real amount received by all Public
Creditors on the conclusion of the war," protest at soldiers'
loss--NG, Jan. 2, 1792. By "A Continental Soldier." *416.

"To the Noblesse and Courtiers of the United States," ironic
editorial for a poet laureate, with satire on Washington's
behavior at levees--NG, Jan. 5, 1793.   417.

("Un-American Newspapers"), editorial vs. Connecticut
Courant and American Mercury of Hartford--NG, Jan. 9,
1793.   418.

("Defense of Clinton"), editorial vs. "Otsego"--NG, Jan. 12,
1793.   419.

("Soldiers' Crimes"), ironic--NG, Jan. 12, 1793. By "A
Continental Soldier."   *420.

("No Great Changes under Federalism"), editorial--NG,
Jan. 12, 1793.   421.

("Praise for Jefferson")--NG, Jan. 16, 1793. By
"Gracchus."   *422.

"Reflections on Balloons," with Freneau poem--in 1795
  Poems as "To Mr. Blanchard"--NG, Jan. 19, 1793.   423.

Aurora (or General Advertiser), Benjamin Franklin Bache,
  editor-publisher, Philadelphia.
("Veterans Will Not Worship One Man"), vs. adulation of
  Washington--Aurora, Jan. 22, 1793. By "Verus."   *424.

"The Upas, or Poison Tree," editorial, NG, Jan. 26,
  1793.   425.

("The Great Legislator"), satire on an assemblyman--Aurora,
  Jan. 29, 1793. By "K.", Freneau pseudonym.   426.

A Farmer series, vs. Washington and Feds: Aurora, Jan.
  29, Feb. 2; NG, Feb. 16, 1793. By "A Farmer."   *

("Washington like a Prince"), satire on "royal" coach--
  Aurora, Jan. 29, 1793. By "A Farmer."   *427.

"Thoughts on Several Subjects", editorial on monarchists,
  titles, equality, sycophants, etc. --NG, Jan. 30, 1793. 428.

("Levees and Equality"), indirect criticism of Washington, in
  "Slender" style--NG, Feb. 2, 1793. By "A Farmer."*429.

("American Ingratitude to French Soldiers"), protest vs. non-
  payment of salaries--NG, Feb. 6, 1793. By "An
  American."   *430.

("Titles for Servants and Slaves"), retort to "A Cit." in GUS
  --NG, Feb. 6, 1793. By "A Brother Cit."   *431.

funding system--NG, March 9, 1793. By "The Voice
of the People."   *442.

("Public-Debt Evils")--NG, March 9, 1793. By "Gracchus."
                                                            *443.

("Army Looseness"), ironic slap at Knox, NG, March 13,
1793. By "Sid Hemet Benengeli."[6]   *444.

"Seasonable Reflections," editorial on ambition in officials--
NG, March 16, 1793.   445.

("Louis's Execution Justified")--NG, March 20, 1793. By
"A Republican," Freneau pseudonym.   446.

("Editorial Motives"), vs. "interested editing," of Fenno in
particular--NG, March 20, 1793. By "Monitor."   *447.

("Louis's Death"), editorial justification--NG, March 20,
1793.   448.

("Concern for Louis, Sign of Royalty"), editorial--NG, March
20, 1793.   449.

("Aristocrats and Priests vs. Deists and Atheists"), defense
of deists and atheists as less dangerous--editorial filler--
NG, March 27, 1793.   450.

"A scrap of Modern Antifoederalism"--anti-fed plot to gain
power--editorial filler--NG, March 27, 1793.   451.

("Treasury Surplus and Debt"), editorial suggestion to buy
bonds with surplus--NG, March 27, 1793.   452.

("Hamilton's Congress Friends Own Bank Stock"), editorial
hint that twenty-five congressmen had shares--NG, March
27, 1793.   453.

Timon series, vs. Hamilton: NG, March 27, April 13,
1793. By "Timon."   *

("Hamilton was Guilty"), passionate argument--NG, March
27, 1793. By "Timon."   *454.

"On Giants", editorial filler--NG, March 30, 1793.   456.

"Inventions and Improvements", editorial on Leslie's
inventions--see NG, Feb. 13, 23, 1793--NG, March 30,
1793.   .   457.

("Values in Free Presses--Aristocratic Grief for Louis"),
editorials--NG, March 30, 1793.   458.

("Flaws in Hamilton's Report"), further attempt to prove
Hamilton's guilt in misapplying funds, with criticism of
national bank and public debt--NG, April 13, 1793. By
"Timon."   *459.

"Guillotine," editorial filler--NG, April 13, 1793.   460.

("Louis's Fate, Deserved")--NG, April 17, 1793. By
"Scevola."   *461.

("French are Better than Britons"), review of British cruelty--
NG, April 20, 1793. By "The Spirit of MDCCLXXVI."
                                                          *462.

("War Unnatural, Instigated by Kings"), editorial reply to
    Fox--NG, April 20, 1793.   463.

An Old Soldier series: NG April 20; Aurora, April 25, (in NG,
    April 27); NG, May 4, 8, 11, 22; Aurora, June 7;
    NG, June 8, 1793.   *

("Brutal Britain, Humane France"), evidently Freneau's
    first use of "Old Soldier"--NG, April 20, 1793. By "An
    Old Soldier."   *464.

("Church Bells Should be Close to the Ground")--Aurora,
    April 22, 1793. By "K.", Freneau pseudonym.   *465.

("American Unfairness to France")--NG, April 24, 1793.
    By "Warren."   *466.

"Modern explanation of a few terms, commonly misunderstood"
    --editorial satire on Feds--NG, April 24, 1793.   467.

("Let's Welcome Genet"), NG, April 24, 1793. By "A
    Freeman."   *468.

("Our Duty to France and Genet")--Aurora, April 25; NG,
    April 27, 1793. By "An Old Soldier."   *469.

("Sycophantic Writers"), editorial--NG, May 1, 1793.   470.

"Enumeration of the Extirpations of Man, since the introduction
    of Fanaticism"--editorial filler--NG, May 1, 4, 1793. 471.

("Praise for France")--NG, May 4, 1793. By "An Old
82

Soldier." *472.

("Honoring Louis is Un-American"), retort to Paine--
Aurora, May 8, 1793. By "Truth." *473.

("British Cruelty and American Pusillanimity")--NG, May 8,
1793. By "An Old Soldier." *474.

("Brissot's Nouveau Voyage dans les Etats Unis"), translated
extract submitted by "X.", with editorial "Remarks"
defending Joseph Reed from charge of persecuting Quakers
--NG, May 8, 1793. 475.

("The French Revolution"), defense--NG, May 11, 1793.
By "An Old Soldier." *476.

("Impolite British Here"), scorn for Britons' insolence and
hatred of France--NG, May 11, 1793. By "A Hint". *477.

("Pope's Control of Rome"), editorial scorn for Catholic
superstition--NG, May 11, 1793. 478.

("France and Her People"), defense--NG, May 11, 15, 1793.
By "A Citizen of the United States." 7,000-8,000 words.
*479.

("Support France!")--NG, May 18, 1793. By "A Citizen."
*480.

("Canal Company's Invasion of Property Rights")--NG, May
18, 1793. By "R. S." (Robert Slender?) *481.

("American Affection for France"),[7] praise for Genet, criticism
of city's merchants, who supported neutrality, a sneer for

the President's proclamation of impartiality and his "royal demeanor"--NG, May 22, 1793. By "An Old Soldier." *482.

("British Sailors' Brutality to French Sailors")--Aurora, May 23, 28, 1793. By "A Citizen." *483.

("Government Ingratitude to Soldiers"), dream essay with poetic epitaph--NG, May 25, 1793. *484.

("American Gratitude to France")--NG, May 25, 1793. By "A Friend to Peace and Mankind." *485.

"Extract of a letter from Montgomery county", on evils of public office--NG, June 5, 1793. By "R. S." (Robert Slender?) *486.

("Americans in French Service"), protest at arrest of American sailors on Citizen Genet, editorial--NG, June 5, 1793. 487.

("The Moon"), editorial speculation on moon's air, seas, people, mountains, etc.--NG, June 5, 1793. 488.

("The Genet Civic Feast"), satire on neutrality proclamation and "dangers" of favoring the French--Aurora, June 7, 1793. By "An Old Soldier." *489.

("Truth and Principles, Not Men"), slap at growth of aristo-cratic and monarchial fashions--NG, June 8, 1793. By "An Old Soldier." *490.

Cool Reflections relative to the French Revolution series:
  NG, June 8, 12, 15, 19, 22, 1793. By "Philadelphus."
                                                                 *

"Cool Reflections" No. I, that Louis deserved to die--NG,
  June 8, 1793. By "Philadelphus."   *491.

"Authentic extract of a letter from a gentleman in Philadelphia to his correspondent in New-York, June 7th, 1793"--
  Tory gloats over Whigs--probably a hoax--NG, June 8,
  1793.   *492.

"Cool Reflections" No. II, on moral need of gratitude to
  France--NG, June 12, 1793. By "Philadelphus."   *493.

("Philadelphia Celebrations of King's Birthday"), editorial
  protest--NG, June 12, 1793.   494.

("Are We Neutral?"), satiric questions on neutrality proclamation, arrest of American sailors fighting for France,
  and holding western forts by Britain--Aurora, June 14,
  1793. By "A Farmer."   *495.

"Cool Reflections" No. III, on American sympathy for France
  --NG, June 15, 1793. By "Philadelphus."   *496.

("Help France Now"), protest at smug attitude of many
  Americans--NG, June 15, 1793. By "Alcanor."   *497.

"The Proclamation", editorial satire on proclamation and
  merchants who supported it--NG, June 15, 1793.   498.

("The Royal Washington Administration"), ironic satire--NG,

June 15, 1793. By "John Bull."   *499.

("Protest at Use of Private Pseudonym"), aimed at "illegal"
  use of "An Old Soldier" (Aurora, June 15)-- Aurora, June
  17, 1793. By "An Old Soldier." (The "criminal" apolo-
  gized June 19.)   *500.

"Cool Reflections" No. IV, on American good will to France
  --NG, June 19, 1793. By "Philadelphus."   *501.

"Extract of a letter, from a gentleman in this city to his
  friend in Alexandria, dated 1st June, 1793," satire on
  local college graduation exercises--NG, June 19, 1793.
                                                              *502.

("Government Mystery"), ironic satire--NG, June 19,
  1793. By "Mercator."   *503.

("Defense of 'Veritas'"), reply to "A Friend to Peace," who
  had replied to "Veritas," critic of our foreign policy
  (probably John Beckley), in NG of June 1-12--NG, June
  19, 1793. By "Observator."   *504.

"Cool Reflections" No. V, on French Revolution as test of
  American love of liberty--NG, June 22, 1793. By
  "Philadelphus."   *505.

("Praise for A Friend to Peace"), ironic satire--NG, June
  26, 1793. By "A Brother-Tory."   *506.

("Old Soldier II, an Aborigine?"), satire on "illegal" user
  of the pseudonym, praise for France--Aurora, June 26,
  1793. By "An Old Man."   *507.

("The Declaration of Independence"), editorial--NG, July 3,
   1793.   508.

("Lovers of Britain"), protest at insults to officers of
   L'Ambuscade in New York--NG, July 3, 1793. By "An
   American."   *509.

("Sources of Monarchy"), with slap at the "royalty" of the
   administration--NG, July 3, 1793. By "Timon."   *510.

"Extract of a letter from a gentlemen in Philadelphia, to his
   Correspondent in New-York, dated 26th of June, 1793",
   protest at ship William case, of prize taken by Citizen
   Genet, then seized by American soldiers by President's
   order--probably a hoax--NG, July 6, 1793.   *511.

("Government Secrecy--Pacificus's Defense of France's
   Enemies"), vs. Hamilton's "Pacificus" letters defending
   neutrality policy in GUS--NG, July 6, 1793. By "Timon."
                                                                 *512.

("British Emissaries"), condemnation of Duché, for France
   and liberty--NG, July 10, 1793. By "Virginius
   Americanus."   *513.

("The Little Democrat Case"), criticism of Washington's
   attitude on arming French privateers in American ports,
   with encouragement to Genet to "act with firmness", like
   an editorial--NG, July 10, 1793. By "Juba."   *514.

"Letter from a tory in Philadelphia to a tory in London,
   dated July 8, 1793", gloating over breaking French-Amer-
   ican friendship--probably a hoax--Aurora, July 11, 1793.

By "Brother Tory." *515.

("Defense of the African Church")--NG, July 13, 1793. By
"A Friend to Truth." *516.

("Washington's Good Intent"), approval of President's explanation of proclamation to Salem citizens (NG, July 3)--
NG, July 13, 1793. By "Taphna." *517.

("Defense of Genet"), retort to "X. Y. " (probably Wither-
spoon), whom Freneau evidently thought to be "A. B. "
(Andrew Brown/ ? /editor of Federal Gazette, where "X. Y. "
appeared)--NG, July 13, 1793. By "Paulus. " *518.

"A New Political Creed--for the use of all whom it may
concern", satire on foreign policy, editorial--NG, July 13,
1793. 519.

("British Treatment of American Ships"), editorial protest--
NG, July 13, 1793. 520.

("British Impertinence"), editorial on letter from Kingston,
Jamaica, warning vs. rash publications--NG, July 13,
1793. 521.

("Advice to Balloonist Decker"), writ in 1789 just before the
balloon burned up--NG, July 17, 1793. 522.

("Policy toward France"), criticism of policy, the Little
Democrat case, government secrecy, etc. --NG, July 17,
1793. By "Alcanor." *523.

("Washington's Lost Popularity"), advice to President, to

88

favor France and be popular--NG, July 17, 1793. By
"Philogenet."   *524.

("Defamation of Foreigners"), retort to "X. Y. junior" in
Federal Gazette-- NG, July 20, 1793. By "Paulus." *525.

("The French Treaty Still Holds"), reply to "Pacificus"
(Hamilton), quote from Burlamqui--NG, July 20, 1793.
By "Turgot."   *526.

("Defense of the Theater"), on respectability's disapproval
of the stage, yet approval of circus--NG, July 20, 1793.
By "A Friend to Consistency."   *527.

("Retort to Metellus"), to "Metellus" (Hamilton), exchange
of wit, with sneer, "You must be a mongrel,"possibly
at Hamilton's birth--Aurora, July 23, 1793. By "Juba."
                                                     *528.

The American Daily Advertiser, John Dunlap, editor-publisher, Philadelphia. ADA

("Pacificus's Errors"), on obligation to observe treaties--
ADA, July 27, 1793. By "An Old Soldier."   *529.

("Public Censure of Washington"), from Charleston Daily
Advertiser of July 12, but in Freneau's style--letter dated
"Charleston, July 4"; the 8-day interval seems improbable,
if letter was writ in Charleston--evidently a hoax; Freneau's
brother Peter could get letter published for him, to give
impression that opposition was countrywide--NG, July 27,
1793. By "A Citizen."   *530.

("Let Congress be Convened on French Treaty"), with slap
   at Hamilton--NG, July 27, 1793. By "Juba."   *531.

("The Right of the Poor to Discuss Public Affairs"), satire
   on idea that only rich should discuss public matters--NG,
   July 31, 1793. By "L."   *532.

("On the Influence of Great Names"), dream essay, emphasizing case of Henfield, tried for fighting for France--NG,
   July 31, 1793. By "Timon."   *533.

("Owners' Rights in Canal Land"), denial of canal makers'
   right to take land arbitrarily--NG, Aug. 3, 1793. By
   "Considerator."   *534.

("Henfield's Acquittal"), editorial--NG, Aug. 3, 1793.   535.

"Reflections on several subjects", editorial on the dominance
   of money, the decline of poetry--NG, Aug. 3, 1793.   536.

("Political Thoughts"), editorial on courts' intimidation of
   juries, the proclamation's unpopularity, need of agriculture's
   voice in government--NG, Aug. 7, 1793.   537.

("Give Wide Publicity to Judges' Opinions"), protest at copy-
   right pamphlets and limited circulation of opinions in state-
   suability case--NG, Aug. 10, 1793. By "A Citizen of the
   United States." ("P. Q.", NG, Aug. 14, denied this and
   "Citizen" retracted, NG, Aug. 28).   *538.

("Defense of Genet's Proposed Appeal to the People")--NG,
   Aug. 17, 1793. By "Alcanor."   *539.

("Federalist Enemies of the United States"), warning to
President to beware--NG, Aug. 17, 1793. By "An
American." *540.

("Editorial Reflections")--on rulers and people, government
and general happiness, monopolies, speculation, Britain
and France--NG, Aug. 17, 1793. Clearly editorial,
though under "Communications from unknown Correspondents." 541.

"Advertisement Extraordinary," editorial defense of Genet's
supposed appeal to American people--NG, Aug. 21,
1793. 542.

"To Mr. B------", humurous address to Aeronaut Blanchard,
probably, with "directions" how to fly among the stars--
NG, Aug. 21, 1793. By "An Old Almanac-Maker."[8] 543.

("Let Governors Omit Titles"), editorial--NG, Aug. 21,
1793. 544.

("Let Congress Decide on Genet"), with criticism of
Gouverneur Morris, government secrecy, and foreign
policy--NG, Aug. 21, 1793. By "Juba." *545.

("The Problem of Peace with Britain--the Popular Preference
for France")--NG, Aug. 24, 1793. By "A Traveller,"
Freneau pseudonym. 546.

Hamlet series: NG, Aug. 28, 31, 1793. By "Hamlet." *

("Our Duty to Genet and France"), passionate defense--NG,

Aug. 28, 1793. By "Hamlet." *547.

("Britain's Sins and Influence in America"), with poetic
   passion--NG, Aug. 31, 1793. By "Hamlet." *548.

("France and England"), editorial for France, vs. our foreign
   policy and secrecy--NG, Aug. 31, 1793. 549.

("Washington's Innocence"), ironic review of reasons for
   people's disillusionment in the President, fake defense
   of him--NG, Sept. 7, 1793. By "Decius." *550.

"Jersey-Coast Inlets", nautical description, editorial filler--
   NG, Sept. 11, 1793. 551.

"Reflections on several Subjects," editorial on Feds, funding
   systems, speculation, etc.--NG, Sept. 11, 1793. Contains
   last 4 lines from Freneau's "Rising Glory of America."
   552.

("The Eve of Monarchy's Fall"), editorial--NG, Sept. 11,
   1793. 553.

"Brief Reflections, on Several Subjects", editorial on
   aristocracy, lovers of wealth and nobility, government
   critics--NG, Sept. 14, 1793. 554.

"Dialogue"--Sun and Moon talk of lie that Earth and Mercury
   found about the Sun (allegory of Fenno?)--NG, Sept. 18,
   1793. *555.

("A Soldier-Cheater"), evidently attack on Elias Boudinot,
   congressman from Elizabethtown, for buying depreciated

due bills and selling at higher prices--NG, Sept. 21, 1793. By "A Soldier." *556.

"Dialogue between a Citizen of Philadelphia, and a Jersey Farmer (ten miles from town)", rebuke to rejecters of refugees from the yellow fever--NG, Sept. 28, 1793. *557.

Philanthropos series: NG, Oct. 2, 12, 1793. On predestination. By "Philanthropos." *

("Predestination Preachers"), criticism of preachers who fled from the yellow fever--NG, Oct. 2, 1793. By "Philanthropos." *558.

"From the Archives of the city of Barrataria, 1693", dialog satire on doctors who fled the fever epidemic--NG, Oct. 5, 1793. *559.

("Defense of the Stage"), reply to preacher's attack--NG, Oct. 9, 1793. By "Consistency." *560.

("Predestination"), reply to a preacher, J. B. Smith, ridicule of predestination--NG, Oct. 12, 1793. By "Philanthropos." *561.

("French Insurrections Caused by Monarchial Gold"), editorial with original verse--NG, Oct. 12, 1793. 562.

("The Service of a Free Press to Freedom"), valedictory editorial--NG, Oct. 19, 1793. By "A Free Press." 563.

("Hamilton's Prejudices"), protest, under "Remarks" below Hamilton's condemnation of Andrew Fraunces--editorial, NG

Oct. 26, 1793. 564.

("The Argument for Genet"), Aurora, Dec. 23, 1793. By
"An Old Soldier." *565.

("Genet and Randolph"), further defense of Genet--Aurora,
Dec. 27, 1793. By "An Old Soldier." *566.

1794

("Quakers' Opposition to the Theater"), ironic defense,
Aurora, Jan. 2, 1794. By "Peter Pasquin." *567.

("Bache, Join Fenno!"), ironic--Aurora, June 12, 1794.
By "Pluto." *568.

Monmouth News-Paper, title of broadside proposal for paper
to be called "The Monmouth Gazette, and East-Jersey
Intelligencer (never published), dated "Mount-Pleasant,
July 4, 1794." Signed "Philip Freneau." See Leary,
American Literature, Nov., 1934. Leary. 569.

("Jay's Faults")--Aurora, Nov. 18, 1794. By "Philo-Republicanus." *570.

Timothy Tinker series, on Democratic societies: Aurora,
Dec. 29, 1794; Jan. 27, 1795. By "Timothy Tinker." *

("The Destruction of the Democratic Societies"), to president
of the Pennsylvania Democratic Society, in "Slender"
style--Aurora, Dec. 29, 1794. From New Jersey, by
"Timothy Tinker." *571.

94

The Monmouth Almanac for the Year M, DCC, XCV-- "Printed
and Sold by P. Freneau" at Middletown-Point, N.J. Un-
paged--so articles are here listed in order of appearance,
omitting some tables and short items. BAL, Paltsits,
Leary. MA.

"The Anatomy of Man's Body, as supposed to be governed
by the XII Constellations, or signs of the Zodiac."
MA.   572.

"Particulars relative to the Bastille of France." MA.   573.

"Of the Planetary System." MA.   574.

"Indian Corn." MA.   575.

"The harmless Incendiary," a story. MA.   576.

"On North-East Storms." MA.   577.

"Of the two ancient cities that have been discovered buried
under the earth"--about Herculaneum and Pompeia.
MA.   578.

"Of the French Calendar." MA.   579.

"Strict discipline observed in the Prussian Armies."
MA.   580.

"On Dogs." MA.   581.

"A Remarkable Imposition," long anecdote. MA.   582.

"A true and faithful account of the Ugly Club, in Charleston
(S. C.) and their manner of seducing strangers into their
club"--from DA, April 5, 1790, revised and enlarged.
MA.   583.

"Advantages of using oxen on farms in preference to horses."
MA.   584.

"Philosophical speculation," on life in the moon. MA. 585.

"Discourse upon Barbers' Poles," from DA, Nov. 1, 1790.
enlarged. MA.   586.

"On Law," that law is not justice. MA.   587.

1795

("Praise for Monarchists"), ironic--Aurora, Jan. 6, 1795.[9]
By "Benedict Arnold."   *588.

("Fenno's Love of Aristocrats")--Aurora, Jan. 10, 1795.
By "E.", Freneau pseudonym. Uses Freneau term,
"Pomposo's dull printer."   *589.

("Fenno's Labors for Democracy"), ironic--Aurora, Jan. 12,
1795. By "A Democrat."   *590.

("What of the Feds, now a Minority?"), from "correspondent"
--Aurora, Jan. 13, 1795.   *591.

("Royal Aims of Federalists"), retort to Fenno--Aurora,
Jan. 14, 1795. By "W."   *592.

("The Title Faction")--<u>Aurora,</u> Jan. 16, 1795. By "Fellow
   Citizen. "   *593.

("Wilcocks, Enemy of Democrats")--<u>Aurora,</u> Jan. 19, 1795.
   By "Puff. "   *594.

("Courage, Democratic Societies!"), in "Slender" style--
   <u>Aurora,</u> Jan. 27, 1795. By "Timothy Tinker. "   *595.

("Wilcocks, America's Blessing"), satire by "correspondent"
   --<u>Aurora,</u> Feb. 2, 1795.   *596.

("The Right to Form Societies")--<u>Aurora,</u> Feb. 7, 1795.
   By "Zenas. "   *597.

("Wilcocks's Mighty Reply")--<u>Aurora,</u> Feb. 9, 1795. By
   "Alcanor. "   *598.

("Treaty Powers--Hamilton's Resignation")--two short essays
   by a "correspondent"--<u>Aurora,</u> Feb. 10, 1795.   *599.

"A Dialogue between Pettifogger and Weathercock", satire
   on government attitude toward Whiskey Rebellion, and plan
   to unseat Gallatin--<u>Aurora,</u> Feb. 13, 1795.   *600.

("Things Not to be Thankful For"), satire on Feds--<u>Aurora,</u>
   Feb. 18, 1795. By "Tom of the Tap-Room. "   *601.

("Defense of poem, 'Aristocracy'")--<u>Aurora,</u> Feb. 24, 1795.
   by "A Real Republican. "   *602.

("Beware Constitution Changes")--<u>Aurora,</u> Feb. 24, 1795.

By "A Watchman."   *603.

("Jay's Peace Toast")--Aurora, Feb. 26, 1795. By
    "Philanthropos."   *604.

("Hamilton's Faults")--Aurora, March 3, 1795. By
    "Puff."   *605.

"To William Wilcocks, Esq. the renowned Knight of New-
    York City"--comic satire--Aurora, March 5, 1795. By
    "Don Quixotte."   *606.

("Theaters Better than Lotteries")--Aurora, March 23, 1795.
    By "Momus."   *607.

("Government Religious Proclamations"), criticism--Aurora,
    March 28, 1795. By "Tom of the Tap-Room."   *608.

Yorick series, defense of "Franklin,"who had criticized Jay
    Treaty:[10] Aurora, April 30, May 6, 16, 1795. By "Yorick." *

("A. B.'s Ignorance"), ridicule of "Franklin's" critic, with
    Pope quote--Aurora, April 30, 1795. By "Yorick." *609.

Jersey Chronicle, Mount Pleasant, N.J., Philip Freneau,
    editor-publisher-printer, 1795-96. Leary, Paltsits.
    JC.

"To the Public"--editorial on policy--JC, May 2, 1795.
    Leary.   610.

("The Jay Treaty"), editorial--JC, May 2, 1795.   611.

98

"Observations on the Treaty with Great Britain", editorial,
JC, May 2, 1795. 612.

("A. B., a Federalist"), also defense of Jefferson, with Pope
(?) quote--Aurora, May 6, 1795. By "Yorick." *613

"On Monarchy," editorial with poetic epitaph to Colonel
Count Donop, Hessian buried at Red Bank, N. J. --JC,
May 9, 1795. 614.

("Principles, Not Men"), editorial vs. birthday celebrations--
JC, May 9, 1795. 615.

("Jefferson's Letter Misinterpreted"), retort to "A. B."--
Aurora, May 16, 1795. By "Yorick." *616.

"Observations on Monarchy", editorial--JC, May 16,
1795. 617.

("Peace Prospects with Indians")--editorial, JC, May 23,
1795. 618.

Tomo Cheeki series: JC, May 23, 30, June 6, 13, 20,
July 4, 11, 18, 25, Aug. 1, 8, 15, 29, Sept. 12, Oct.
17, 31, 1795. Oct. 31 continues Oct. 17. Leary,
except note of Oct. 31 continuation.

"Tomo Cheeki, the Creek Indian in Philadelphia"--introduction,
of Creek's visit to make a treaty, Tomo's notes, their
"translation"--JC, May 23, 1795. In TP, March 15,
1797. 619.

99

("Perkin's Nail Machine"), satire on claims by Perkins of
Newbury-port--JC, May 30, 1795. By "A New-Jersey
Forge Man." *620.

"Maxims and Observations, partly original and partly extract-
ed from different authors", on government, history, etc.--
editorial--JC, May 30, 1795. 621.

"On the branch of Government denominated Executive,"
editorial--JC, May 30, 1795. 622.

"Tomo Cheeki," No. I--"Reflections, on my first entering
the great City of the White Men," JC, May 30, 1795.
In TP, March 17, 1797. Leary. 623.

"Tomo Cheeki," No. II, "Consolatory advice to my brother
Nantounawaw (of the embassy) who had applied to be made
a member of a Philosophical Society"--satire on American
Philosophical Society--JC, June 6, 1795. In TP, March
29, 1797. Leary. 624.

("Pro-English Reviewer Wrong"), vs. GUS article--Aurora,
June 6, 1795. By "An American." *625.

("Coming European Convulsions"), editorial--JC, June 13,
1795. 626.

"Tomo Cheeki," No. III, "A Piece written in the night--
to which is added a short Dream"--defense of Indians,
criticism of whites and suspicion--JC, June 13, 1795. In
TP, March 24, 1797. Leary. 627.

"Tomo Cheeki," No. IV, "A short talk on Drunkenness"--
JC, June 20, 1795. From DA, Sept. 1, 1790. In TP,
April 17, 1797. Leary. 628.

("Senate Treaty Mystery"), editorial protest--JC, June 27,
1795. 629.

"Tomo Cheeki," No. V, "Containing certain Indian Notions
and Reflections"--on whites' quitting rural ways, change,
antiquity, and Indians' decline--JC, July 4, 1795. In TP,
April 3, 1797. Leary. 630.

("The Declaration of Independence"), editorial--JC, July 4,
1795. 631.

("The Growing American Navy and Naval Resources"),
editorial on restricting supplies to Britain, to force better
treatment in commerce with France--JC, July 4, 1795.
632.

"On some of the Principles of American Republicanism",
editorial filler--JC, July 4, 1795. In TP, May 5,
1797. 633.

"Tomo Cheeki," No. VI, "To the Big Loom, a white man
of this Village," tale of Moncachtape's journey to Pacific
and back--JC, July 11, 1795. In TP, May 5, 1797.
Leary. 634.

("Fenno's Treaty Profits"), vs. Fenno's selling copies of
Jay Treaty, yet opposing publication--Aurora, July 16,
1795. By "Momus." *635.

"Tomo Cheeki," No. VII, "Written about Midnight", pity for
   whites and praise for Indian free life--JC, July 18, 1795.
   In TP, March 20, 1797. Leary (in TP, March 29, 1790).
                                                        636.

"Tomo Cheeki," No. VIII, ("An Indian's Rights"), dream
   of oration by an Indian head--JC, July 25, 1795. From
   NG, Jan. 12, 1792. In TP, June 2, 1797. Leary.
                                                        637.

"Tomo Cheeki" No. IX ("Superstition and Horse Shoes"), JC,
   Aug. 1, 1795. Same as "Discourse on Horse Shoes",
   DA, Sept. 17, 1790. In TP, May 29, 1797. Leary.
                                                        638.

"Tomo Cheeki" No. X ("Civilization's Evils")--JC, Aug. 8,
   1795. In TP, May 12, 1797. Leary.   639.

("Treaty Defenders Camillus and Curtius"), on Hamilton's
   and Webster's writings--Aurora, Aug. 12, 1795. By
   "E.", Freneau pseudonym.   640.

"Tomo Cheeki" No. XI ("The Retired Sea Captain")--JC,
   Aug. 15, 1795. From "A Speech on a New Subject," DA,
   June 29, 1790. Leary.   641.

("British Advantages in the Treaty"), editorial--JC, Aug. 22,
   1795.   642.

"On the Ingratitude of Republics", denial of idea, with slap
   at the ingratitude of the government to veterans, editorial--
   JC, Aug. 29, 1795.   643.

"Tomo Cheeki" No. XII ("The Golden Age")--JC, Aug. 29,

1795. In TP, April 7, 1797. Leary.   644.

("Tory Merchant Backers of the Treaty"), satire--Aurora,
    Aug. 31, 1795. By "One of the Swinish Multitude,"
    favorite expression of "Robert Slender."   *645.

("Biography of William Bradford, Jr."), DA, Sept. 1, 1795,
    from Argus. By "L."   645a.

"The Devil upon Two Sticks in Philadelphia. --A Fragment",
    writ in yellow fever epidemic of 1793, satire on doctors
    and aristocrats--JC, Sept. 5, 1795. (Foote's Devil upon
    Two Sticks was then a popular farce.)   *646.

"Tomo Cheeki" No. XIII--"To Hopiniyahie, an Indian Woman
    on the south side of the river O-conee," on vanities of
    whites--JC, Sept. 12, 1795. In TP, April 12, 1797.
    Leary.   647.

"The treaty unmasked," editorial vs. Article IX, allowing
    landholders in both countries to continue as such, favoring
    British holders of land in America--JC, Sept. 12, 1795.
                                                          648.

("A Giant Skeleton"), editorial on bones found in South
    Carolina--JC, Sept. 12, 1795.   649.

"The Circle of Human Life," evidently an editorial paraphrase
    from Gratian--JC, Sept. 26, 1795. In TP, May 8, 1797.
                                                          650.

"The Recantation of a Tory of 1776," satire on treaty and
    the kingly ways of Washington--JC, Oct. 10, 1795. By
    "Timothy Turnpenny."   *651.

103

("Defense of Washington"), reply to "Timothy Turnpenny" in the same weekly issue, unlikely timing, following the attack directly--JC, Oct. 10, 1795. By "An Old Soldier." *652.

"Tomo Cheeki" No. XIV, "A Dream in a Dark Night of the Hunting Moon"--on whites' eventual self-destruction, their replacement by a more benevolent creature--JC, Oct. 17, 1795. In TP, April 21, 1797. Leary.   653.

"View of our European Commerce," editorial--JC, Oct. 24, 1795.   654.

"Tomo Cheeki" No. XV, actually continuation of No. XIV-- JC, Oct. 31, 1795. In TP, April 28, 1797. Omitted by Leary.   655.

("The English and the French"), editorial--JC, Nov. 7, 1795.   656.

"Captain Hudson's Discovery of the river at New-York, that now bears his name," editorial filler--JC, Nov. 21, 1795.   657.

"Hispaniola," editorial description, probably from personal observation--JC, Nov. 21, 1795.   658.

"A Political Creed", editorial, for equal rights, tolerance, representative government, etc.---JC, Dec. 5, 1795. 659.

("France is Not Appreciated"), to President, with reference to his recent address to Congress--Aurora, Dec. 15, 1795. (Slightly altered, with signature removed, in JC, Jan. 30,

1796--q.v.) By "An Old Soldier."   *660.

("The Paris Royal Uprisings"), editorial--JC, Dec. 19,
1795.   661.

("Republican Liberties and Tendencies to Monarchy"),
editorial--JC, Dec. 26, 1795.   662.

"Solomon and the queen of Sheba," editorial filler--JC, Dec.
26, 1795.   663.

"Grand Epochs of Europe," editorial condensation from "a
late writer" on chivalry, religion, commerce, and politics
--JC, Dec. 26, 1795.   664.

1796

("Praise for Washington"), editorial condensation of a "letter
from Philadelphia"--JC, Jan. 16, 1796.   665.

("A New Kind of Paper"), editorial on Biddis's invention of
paper partly from sawdust--JC, Jan. 30, 1796.   666.

Republication of No. 660, from Aurora, by "An Old Soldier",
but with a change in the concluding sentence, and without
the signature--JC, Jan. 30, 1796. [11]   667.

("Randolph's Vindication"), editorial for Randolph, critical
of Washington--JC, Feb. 6, 1796.   668.

("Washington City"), editorial criticism--JC, March 12,
1796.   669.

105

"Reflections on different Subjects", editorial on British "friendship," American political idolatry, treaties, banks, speculation, etc.--JC, March 19, 1796. 670.

"War! War!! War!!!"--ironic, on dire results of non-ratification of the Jay Treaty--Aurora, March 23, 1796. By "A Friend to the Treaty." *671.

("British Fears of Revolution"), editorial, original verse-- JC, April 16, 1796. 672.

("Non-Ratification Disasters"), satire on merchants' fears (from NYA)--Aurora, April 21, 1796. By "A Friend to the Treaty." *673.

("The Mighty Wilcocks"), satire with quote from Henry IV, and other literary references, "from a correspondent"-- Aurora, April 28, 1796. *674.

"Proposals for Printing and Publishing a Gazette for the Country, to be entitled the Register of the Times"-- project never achieved, to be published by New York Diary-- JC, April 23, 1796. Signed "The Editors of the Diary." *675.

("Worship of Washington--Abuse of Republicans"), editorial with original verse--JC, April 30, 1796. 676.

"An Apologue", story of Greeks who visited moon, editorial filler--JC, April 30, 1796. In TP, March 22, 1797. 677.

"A Jewish Tradition", story of how apparent injustice may be

justice, editorial filler--JC, April 30, 1796. In TP,
   March 22, 1797.   678.

("Editor's Farewell")--JC died because unprofitable--JC,
   April 30, 1796. Signed "Philip Freneau." Leary.   679.

The Argus, Thomas Greenleaf, editor-publisher, New York.
   NYA.

("Defense of the Jersey Chronicle and Freneau"), retort to
   criticism in GUS (May 7)--NYA, May 14, 1796. By "G."
   Freneau pseudonym.   680.

"The French Victories"), mock horror from "a correspondent"
   --Aurora, July 29, 1796.   *681.

("Retort to Phocion"), ridicule of W. L. Smith's revival of
   the 1792 charges of Hamilton, from "a correspondent"--
   Aurora, Nov. 3, 1796.   *682.

("A Change in Feds"), on advocacy of war with France--
   Aurora, Dec. 24, 1796. By "A Watchman."   *683.

("British Schemes vs. France and Jefferson"), quote from
   Freneau's translation of Robin's Travels (p. 80)--Aurora,
   Dec. 27, 1796. By "An Old Soldier."[12]   684.

1797

("Extravagant Praise of Washington"), satire on state's
   House's reply to governor's address, with Goldsmith quote--
   Aurora, Jan. 6, 1797. By "Semper Idem."   *685.

Simon Steady series, satire on addresses to the President:
Aurora, Feb. 6, 20, 1797. By "Simon Steady."   *

("The F----Fire Company's Address to Washington"), satire
on addresses to the President in his praise, comic tale
of meeting, with verse--Aurora, Feb. 6, 1797. By
"Simon Steady."   *686.

("Condemnation of Adulatory Addresses"), speech by Mr.
Sensible at F----Fire Company meeting--Aurora, Feb. 20,
1797. By "Simon Steady."   *687.

("Defense of Swift"), reply to Callender's American Annual
Register--Aurora, March 9, 1797. By "Candour."   *688.

The Time Piece, and Literary Companion, after Sept. 15,
1797, called The Time Piece, Philip Freneau, editor and
co-publisher with Alexander Menut till Sept. 15, 1797,
with Matthew Davis till Jan. 3, 1798, when Freneau left
New York, though officially a partner till March 21, 1798.
Davis "& Co." continued till June 18, 1798; R. Saunders
published till July 9; John Burk and James Smith published
till the last issue, Aug. 30, 1798. New York, 1797-98.
Paltsits, Leary. TP.

"To the Public", opening editorial on policy--TP, March 13,
1797. By "Philip Freneau." Leary.   689.

"Proposals for Publishing a New Paper, to be entitled The
Time-Piece, and Literary Companion"--TP prospectus,
TP, March 13-22, 1797. By "Philip Freneau."   690.

"Observations on Monarchy," editorial--TP, March 13, 1797.
Same as in JC, May 16, 1795.   691.

New Travels Through North-America, by Claude Robin,
Philadelphia, 1783, translated by Freneau, serialized in
TP: March 15, 17, 20, 22, 27, 29, 31, April 3, 5 , 7,
10, 12, 14, 17, 19, 21, 24, 26, 28, May 1, 3, 1797.
In first number, editor says he was the translator.
Leary, page 433.

Tomo Cheeki essays from JC: TP, March 15 (introduction),
17, 20, 24, 29, April 3, 7, 12, 17, 21, 28, May 5, 12,
22, 29, June 2, 16, 1797. New essays, May 22 and June
16, 1797. Leary lists all separately.

"An Essay on Horses," against cruelty--TP, March 24,
1797. Editorial filler.   692.

"Curious Particulars in the character of the late King of
Prussia, not generally known"--editorial filler, TP,
March 27, 1797.   693.

"Concise Account of the Improvements of the Greeks, and of
the Destruction of their Trade, Power, and Independence"--
editorial filler--TP, April 14, 1797.   694.

"Essay on Beauty," editorial filler--TP, April 24, 1797. 695.

("Synpathy for France"), from "a correspondent," but like
Freneau, with original verse--TP, April 26, 1797.   *696.

("Review of The Secret History of the French Revolution"),

of book by Francis Page--TP, April 26, translated parts
April 28, May 1, 3, 8, 10, 12, 15, 24, 31, 1797.   697.

"Equestrian Exercises at Mr. Ricketts' Circus," with Freneau
poem, in 1809 Poems "Lines Written for Mr. Ricketts"--
TP, May 1, 1797.   698.

"Proposals for Printing...The Secret History of the French
Revolution," offered by TP--TP, May 12, 1797.   699.

("Belief in Ghosts"), with Iliad quote, editorial introduction--
TP, May 22, 1797.   700.

("The Mammoth and Immortality"), new "Tomo Cheeki" essay
--TP, May 22, 1797.   Leary.   701.

("Rushton's Address to Washington"), on pamphlet protesting
Washington's use of slaves, editorial approval--TP, May
26, 1797.   702.

("Jefferson's Letter to Mazzei"), translated from Gazette
Nationale and Paris Moniteur--TP, June 7, 1797.   703.

("War's Horrors"), editorial with verse--TP, June 9, 1797.
                                                    704.

("Causes of Celebrity"), translated from Bonneville--TP,
June 16, 1797.   705.

"Sandy Hook," editorial description, with Dryden quote--TP,
June 16, 1797.   706.

"To Opay-Meeko--(the old man of the Lake) in the Creek

110

country," new "Tomo Cheeki" essay, on nature, moon,
etc.--TP, June 16, 1797.   707.

"Sketches on Different Subjects," editorial on ancient and
modern kings, origin of navies--TP, June 21, 1797.   708.

("Let Us Be Neutral"), editorial on France, with Hudibras
quote--TP, June 23, 1797.   709.

"Madame Lafayette," editorial filler--TP, June 30, 1797.   710.

("World Revolution Inevitable"), editorial with Shakespeare
quote--TP, July 7, 1797.   711.

("Assorted Editorials"), on monarchy's cruelty, British biography, Monroe's toast to peace with France, etc.--TP,
July 21, 1797.   712.

"Ledyard's Travels", on proposal to publish--TP, July 26,
1797. By "Philip Freneau."   713.

("The British Naval Crisis"), including "Banyan Days," on sailors' small ration days, editorial--TP, Aug. 2, 1797.   714.

"The Plan of Plans: being a Serious Address to Both Houses of
Congress," on paying national debt by raising hogs--TP,
Aug. 2, 1797. By "Mat. Moonshine, jun."   *715.

("The Russia-Austria-England Alliance"), translated from
Gazette Nationale--TP, Aug. 7, 9, 11, 14, 16, 1797.   716.

("Parliament's Need of Reform"), editorial--TP, Aug. 9,
1797.   717.

reading shop--TP, Sept. 8, 1797.   728.

"The Old Connecticut Blue Laws (alias, Bloody Laws)",
    editorial filler--TP, Sept. 11, 1797.   729.

("Fenno's Use of Quotations"), bitter editorial--TP, Sept. 11,
    1797.   730.

("Fenno and Porcupine"), editorial warning vs. levities made
    under yellow-fever threat--TP, Sept. 11, 1797.   731.

("Presidential Retirement"), satire on idea that retirement
    means philosophical contemplation, editorial with verse--
    TP, Sept. 11, 1797.   732.

"To the Public", editorial on Matthew Davis's entry into the
    TP partnership, replacing Menut, new plans--TP, Sept. 13,
    1797.   733.

("Minerva's Bias to Foreigners"), editorial slap at Noah
    Webster--TP, Sept. 13, 1797.   734.

("Scurrilous Porcupine"), editorial with original verse, retort
    to Cobbett slur--TP, Sept. 13, 1797.   Leary.   735.

("Porcupine and Fenno"), editorial criticism of their support
    of aristocracy--TP, Sept. 15, 1797.   736.

("Henry the Eighth"), editorial criticism with verse--TP,
    Sept. 15, 1797.   737.

("The Dissolution of French Religious Houses"), editorial, with probable Freneau poem--TP, Sept. 15, 1797.   738.

"The sorrowful petition of U, G, H, to the American Printers, "
comic protest at omission of letters in thought, etc. --TP,
Sept. 15, 1797.   *739.

("Defense of France"), editorial, TP, Sept. 18, 1797.   740.

("The Pope's Recent Tameness"), editorial, TP, Sept. 18,
1797.   741.

("Abusive Porcupine"), editorial with original verse--TP,
Sept. 18, 1797. Leary.   742.

"Ridiculous Distress of a Country Weekly News Printer, "
comic tale--TP, Sept. 20, 1797. By "A Traveller, "
Freneau pseudonym. [13]   743.

("Newspapers' Utility and Difficulties"), editorial with Freneau
poem, "On the Death of a Country Printer"--TP, Sept. 22,
1797. Leary, page 458. Poem in 1795 Poems as "On
the Death of a Republican Printer. "   744.

("Fenno and Royalty"), editorial with verse--TP, Sept. 25,
1797.   745.

("Royal Excesses on the Stage"), editorial--TP, Sept. 25,
1797.   746.

("No French Bribes to Democratic Printers"), editorial with
Freneau poem--TP, Sept. 25, 1797. Leary. Poem much
changed and enlarged, as "To the Democratic Country

114

Editors," in 1809 <u>Poems.</u>   747.

("France Innocent of American Sabotage"), editorial with
    verse--TP, Sept. 25, 1797.   748.

("Evils of Luxury"), editorial introduction--TP, Sept. 27,
    1797.   749.

("Fenno's Denial of Royal Attachment"), editorial with verse--
    TP, Sept. 27, 1797.   750.

("National Enmity Petty"), editorial with verse--TP, Sept.
    27, 1797.   751.

("The Burden of Navies"), editorial--TP, Sept. 27, 1797.
                                                                    752.

("The Failure of the <u>Constitution</u> Launching"), editorial with
    Freneau poem--TP, Sept. 29, 1797. Leary. Poem,
    much changed, in the 1815 <u>Poems</u> as "On the Launching
    of the Frigate Constitution."   753.

("The Soul"), editorial--TP, Sept. 29, 1797.   754.

("American Usurers"), introduction to Freneau poem--TP,
    Sept. 29, 1797. Leary. Poem in 1809 <u>Poems,</u> much
    changed, as "A Usurer's Prayer."   755.

("New-Rich Americans"), editorial with Freneau poem--TP,
    Oct. 2, 1797. Leary. Poem, much changed, in 1809
    <u>Poems</u> as "The Political Weathercock."   756.

("Property as a Voting Basis"), editorial ridicule--TP, Oct. 6,
    1797.   757.

("Retort to Fenno"), editorial with original verse--TP, Oct. 6, 1797. Leary. 758.

("Praise for Burk's Columbiad"), editorial introduction to extracts of epic by John Burk--TP, Oct. 9, 1797. Leary. 759.

("Britain's Attack on Teneriffe"), editorial criticism--TP, Oct. 9, 1797. 760.

("Fenno's Praise of Porcupine"), editorial with verse--TP, Oct. 9, 1797. 761.

"Fools will be meddling"--on collegians' enmity for France-- TP, Oct. 13, 1797. By "G.", Freneau pseudonym. 762.

"Monroe"--praise for Monroe, condemnation of his enemies-- TP, Oct. 13, 1797. By "A Native American." *763.

("Defense of Porcupine"), approval of right to criticize blood-letting--TP, Oct. 16, 1797. By "A Republican," Freneau pseudonym. 764.

("The President's Banquet"), editorial criticism of elaborate presidential feasting--TP, Oct. 16, 1797. 765.

"Political Observations, drawn from the actual State of Things"--editorial on wealth, taxes, naval life, etc.--TP, Oct. 20, 1797. 766.

Hezekiah Salem[14] series: satires of the Connecticut Yankee-- TP, Oct. 23, 25, 31, Nov. 1, 10, 13, 17, 1797. By

"Hezekiah Salem." Leary.

"On the Culture of Pumpkins, by Hezekiah Salem, late of
New England"-- TP, Oct. 23, 1797. Leary (as Oct. 25).
767.

"A Sketch of Biography," TP, Oct. 25, 1797. By "Hezekiah
Salem." Leary. 768.

"First Chapter of the Third Book of Chronicles," editorial
satire of John Adams and Noah Webster--TP, Oct. 25,
1797. 769.

("Continental Wars"), editorial with verse--TP, Oct. 25,
1797. 770.

"Detached Observations and Reflections," editorial on political
vice, old Greece, natural rights, etc.--TP, Oct. 25, 1797.
771.

"Incendiaries", defense of France--TP, Oct. 31, 1797. By
"Hotonthologus." *772.

"Rules how to get through a crowd," comic--TP, Oct. 31,
1797. By "Hezekiah Salem." Leary. 773.

"From Hezekiah Salem's Last Basket", complaint against
housekeeper for moving his books--TP, Nov. 1, 1797.
By "Hezekiah Salem." Leary. 774.

("Republics Not Levellers"), editorial retort to London writer--
TP, Nov. 1, 1797. 775.

("Duelling Should End"), editorial--TP, Nov. 1, 1797. 776.

("Militia, Don't Parade for Adams")--<u>Aurora</u>, Nov. 4, 1797.
By "An Old Soldier." *777.

"A few Words on Duelling", satire--TP, Nov. 10, 1797.
By "Hezekiah Salem." Leary. 778.

("On Equality"), editorial retort to Fenno, for human vs.
property rights--TP, Nov. 10, 1797. By "Universal
Justice." 779.

("The Rough Road to Liberty"), editorial--TP, Nov. 10,
1797. 780.

("Congratulations for Not Parading"), to most of militia, who
did not appear for Adams--<u>Aurora</u>, Nov. 13, 1797. By
"An Old Soldier." *781.

"The Howling House," on Salem's preference for the "music"
of wind blowing around a house--TP, Nov. 13, 1797.
By "Hezekiah Salem." Leary. 782.

("Christianity and Democracy Not Opposed"), editorial retort
to Webster, defense of France--TP, Nov. 13, 1797. 783.

("Military Courage a Mechanism"), editorial--TP, Nov. 13,
1797. 784.

("The Folly of Statues"), editorial introduction to French
account of demolishing a statue--TP, Nov. 15, 1797. 785.

"A Scrap, from a Keg, of Hezekiah Salem's Sermons", urging
small men not to be discouraged because of size--TP, Nov.
118

17, 1797. By "Hezekiah Salem." Leary. 786.

("The British War Habit"), editorial--TP, Nov. 20, 1797.
787.

("The British-New York Evacuation Anniversary"), editorial--
TP, Nov. 24, 1797. 788.

("Ambiguous Adams"), editorial--TP, Nov. 24, 1797. 789.

("Aristocratic Adams"), criticism of the President's answers
to New Jersey Addresses--TP, Nov. 26, 1797. By "A
Republican," Freneau pseudonym. 790.

("The Royalist Revolution in France"), editorial with verse--
TP, Nov. 26, 1797. 791.

("Rousseau's 'Of Deputies or Representatives'"), editorial
comments--TP, Nov. 29, 1797. 792.

("On Echoing Presidential Speeches"), editorial--TP, Nov.
29, 1797. 793.

("Yale College Customs"), editorial criticism of strict rules,
and resultant student capers--TP, Nov. 29, 1797. 794.

("Deported British Jacobins"), editorial retort to Fenno,
defense of deportees--TP, Dec. 4, 1797. 795.

"On Various Modes of Eating," book review of unnamed book--
TP, Dec. 4, 1797. 796.

("British Rules for the Colonies"), editorial criticism,

119

especially of shipping restrictions--TP, Dec. 4, 1797.

        797.

("Restless Royalty"), editorial with verse--TP, Dec. 6,
    1797.   798.

("National Pride"), editorial referring to Zimmerman's book
    on the subject--TP, Dec. 11, 1797. Extracts, Dec. 13,
    1797.   799.

On Imprisonment for Debt series: Dec. 13, 18, 25, 1797.
    By "A. B.", Freneau pseudonym.

"On Imprisonment for Debt," protest, with quote from Shakes-
    peare's Tempest-- TP, Dec. 13, 1797. By "A. B.",
    Freneau pseudonym.   800.

("The European Situation"), criticism of tyranny, editorial
    with verse--TP, Dec. 15, 1797.   801.

"On Imprisonment for Debt" No. II, recommendation of
    benevolent societies' help--TP, Dec. 18, 1797. By
    "A. B."   802.

("That First Ode"), editorial retort to Connecticut Courant,
    on Freneau's first poem in the Book of Odes (TP, Oct.
    16, 1797), criticized as a parody of the first psalm of
    David--TP, Dec. 22, 1797.   803.

("The New Eagle"), introduction to poem, "Address to the
    New Invented Eagle," both satires on a painting by a
    New York doctor, very funny--TP, Dec. 22, 1797. By
    "Jonathan."   *804.

("On Imprisonment for Debt") No. II, untitled--criticism of
easy credit, with plan for inmates to learn a trade and
earn money while confined--TP, Dec. 25, 1797. Unsigned.   805.

1798

Lysander[15]series, vs. Adams and his policy: TP, April 17,
23, May 2, 23, 28, June 6, 8, 11, 15, 18, 1798. By
"Lysander."   *

("Monarchism Not for America")--TP, April 17, 1798. By
"Lysander."   *806.

("Beware of War!")--TP, April 23, 1798. By "Lysander."
                                                              *807.

("Neutrality, Our Natural Policy")--TP, May 2, 1798. By
"Lysander."   *808.

("War and Presidential Leadership")--TP, May 23, 1798.
By "Lysander."   *809.

("Americans in 1776 and Now"), vs. English alliance--Aurora,
May 26, 1798. By "Alfred."   *810.

The New-York Journal, Thomas Greenleaf, publisher-editor,
New York, NYJ.

"Crisis," warning vs. war, from NYA--NYJ, May 26, 1798.
By "A Native American."   *811.

("American Tories")--TP, May 28, 1798. By "Lysander."
                                                              *812.

("British Cruelty")--<u>Aurora</u>, May 30, 1798. By "An
   American."   *813.

"The Political Confab", dialog vs Adams and for France,
   from NYA--NYJ, June 2, 1798. By "A By Stander."
                                                                 *814.

("The XYZ Problem")--TP, June 6, 8, 11, 1798. By
   "Lysander."   *815.

("The Alien Law"), protest--<u>Aurora</u>, June 8, 1798. By
   "Montgomery."   *816.

<u>Democritus</u> series, satire on Adams: <u>Aurora</u>, June 8, 25,
   1798. By "Democritus."   *

("Praise for Adams"), ironic, to "His Serene Highness"--
   <u>Aurora</u>, June 8, 1798, from <u>Carey's United States Record-
   er</u>. By "Democritus."   *817.

("Our Treatment of France")--TP, June 15, 18, 1798. By
   "Lysander."   *818.

"Democracy," with Freneau poem, satire on Porcupine--NYA,
   June 25, 1798. Leary records poem. Poem in 1815
   <u>Poems</u>, enlarged, as "The Royal Cockneys in America--
   1797."   819.

("Spanish Juster than British")--<u>Aurora</u>, June 25, 1798.
   By "Pythagoras."   *820.

("The Adams Policy"), satire--<u>Aurora</u>, June 25, 1798, from
   Carey's <u>Recorder</u>. By "Democritus."   *821.

("An American Bastile?"), satire on Alien Law in "Slender"
   style--Aurora, July 3, 1798. By "Richard Frugal." *822.

("Defense of General Morgan and Governor Mifflin"), to
   Fenno, with slur that he took a bribe--Aurora, July 3,
   1798. By "Fillip."   *823.

"Last Will and Testament of a Democrat, on a Sick Bed in
   the last stages of an Aristocratic Consumption," satire on
   Adams, Congress, and Hamilton--TP, July 4, 1798.
   By "An Old Soldier."   *824.

("Adams's Reply to the Militia"), criticism, to Adams--
   Aurora, July 14, 1798. By "Several of the Militia of
   Morris County." In TP, July 16, 1798.   825.

("The Alien-Sedition Acts")[16], mock fears in "Slender" style--
   Aurora, July 21, 1798. By "Timothy Tremulous." *826.

Sancho series: Aurora, Aug. 3, 4, 21, 1798. By "Sancho."
                                                          *

"More Terror", criticism of book, Proofs of a Conspiracy
   against all the Religions and Governments of Europe, as
   "insufferable trash"--Aurora, Aug. 3, 1798. By "Sancho."
                                                          *827.

("Holcroft's [17] Poem, 'The Hero'")--Aurora, Aug. 4, 1798.
   By "Sancho."   *828.

("Persecution for Political Opinions"), satire on young Fenno
   and Bache's other enemies--Aurora, Aug. 13, 1798. By
   "Obadiah."   *829.

123

("Holcroft's Hugh Trevor")--Aurora, Aug. 21, 1798. By
   "Sancho."   *830.

("Attacks on France"), protest, Aurora, Aug. 28, 1798.
   By "Cato." Dated at "New-Jersey."   *831.

("Enemies of Free Speech"), warning--Aurora, Aug. 29,
   1798. By "Mentor."   *832.

("The Dangerous British Lion"), retort to Boston toast on
   Adams's birthday--Aurora, Nov. 9, 1798. By "William
   Tell."   *833.

("Aspersions on the French")--Aurora, Nov. 9, 1798. By
   "Paley."   *834.

"Reflections on the Recent Conduct of the King of Great-
   Britain", protest at treatment of American ships in the
   West Indies--Aurora, Dec. 5, 1798. Like an editorial.
   By "Columbus."   *835.

("The Senate and President"), satire in "Slender" style--
   Aurora, Dec. 13, 1798. By "Jarzy Blue."   *836.

("Objections to Logan's Service"), satire of Adams and the
   Feds--Aurora, Dec. 26, 1798. By "Gag."   *837.

                            1799
("To the German Federalist"), satire on a critic of Logan--
   Aurora, Jan. 22, 1799. By "Scourge."   *838.

("Death and Funeral of the Gazette of the United States"), mock-

                            124

serious epitaph, based on J. W. Fenno's announcement
of giving up[18] GUS--<u>Aurora</u>, March 9, 1799.   *839.

<u>Robert Slender</u> series: collected (see <u>Letters...of Robert
Slender</u>[19])--<u>Aurora</u>, March 25, 29, April 23, May 3, 7,
16, 20, June 11, 18, 19, July 6 (poem only), Aug. 1, 8,
9, 16, 17, 20, 23, 24, Sept. 3, 11, 27, Oct. 2, 1799;
uncollected--Aug. 6 (by"Slender Thomas"), Sept. 28, Nov.
6, 9, 23, 30, Dec. 4, 1799; Aug. 5, Sept. 10, Oct. 2,
9, Nov. 17, 18, 1800; Feb. 19, 1801. By "Robert
Slender." Leary.

("Rulers Need Not be Just"), satire on Alien-Sedition Laws--
<u>Aurora</u>, March 25, 1799. By "A Monarchist." Leary.
<u>Letters</u>, No. I.   840.

("Fast Proclamations"), rebuke to Adams--<u>Aurora</u>, March
27, 1799. By "An Old Ecclesiastic."   *841.

("Hypocrisy in Kings and the Rich"), --<u>Aurora</u>, March 29,
1799. By "Robert Slender." Leary. <u>Letters</u>, No. II.
                                                      842.

("Aristocrats' Contempt for Poor")--<u>Aurora</u>, April 23, 1799.
By "Robert Slender." Leary. <u>Letters</u>, No. III.   843.

("Federalist Injustice to Radicals")--<u>Aurora</u>, May 3, 1799.
By "Robert Slender". Leary. <u>Letters</u>, No. IV.   844.

("France's Justification")--<u>Aurora</u>, May 7, 1799. By "Robert
Slender." Leary. <u>Letters</u>, No. V.   845.

("Aristocrat, Beast")--<u>Aurora</u>, May 16, 1799. By "Robert

Slender." Leary. Letters, No. VI. 846.

("Party Violence"), satire on Duane's beating and his enemies--
Aurora, May 20, 1799. By "Robert Slender". Leary.
Letters, No. VII. 847.

("Darwin's Poetry"), praise of Erasmus Darwin's work--
Aurora, June 10, 1799. By "W----." *848.

("Fed Reports of French Conspiring"), satire--Aurora, June
11, 1799. By "Robert Slender." Leary. Letters,
No. VIII. 849.

("Dangers in Free Speech"), mock warning to Slender--Aurora,
June 18, 1799. By "Simon Simple," Slender's cousin.
Leary. Letters, No. IX. 850.

("The Feds Feel Justified"), ironic defense--Aurora, June
19, 1799. By "Robert Slender." Leary. Letters, No. XI.
851.

("McKean and Ross"), vs. Ross, candidate for governor--
Aurora, June 28, 1799. By "An Enemy to Deists." *852.

("Ross Unfit to be Governor")--Aurora, June 29, 1799. By
"Veritas." *853.

("The Murderer, Suwarraw"), vs. Russian general, Suwarrow,
whom Feds had praised--Aurora, July 3, 1799. By "No
Federal Suwarraw." *854.

Patriotic poem, by "Martial jun."--Aurora, July 6, 1799.
Leary, p. 312. In Letters, No. XII.

("The Election Drama"), on Feds' royal plans, with Shakespeare quote--Aurora, July 10, 1799. By "Vivat Rex et
Regina."   *855.

("Slender is No Seditious Alien"), reply to "Simon Simple"--
Aurora, Aug. 1, 1799. By "Robert Slender." Leary.
Letters, No. X.   856.

("Alarm over Conspiracies"), mock fears, Aurora, Aug. 6,
1799. By "Slender Thomas," Robert's cousin.   857.

("Shifting Orthodoxy"), on Church's changed attitude to
Catholicism since the French Revolution--Aurora, Aug. 8,
1799. By "Robert Slender." Leary. Letters, No. XIII.
                                                            858.

("A Mistake about American Vessels"), rebuke to State
Department, Aurora, Aug. 9, 1799. By "Robert Slender."
Leary. Letters, No. XIV.   859.

("Vote against Ross"), Aurora, Aug. 13, 1799. By
"Scaevola."   *860.

("A Defense of Ladies' Fashions"), retort to Editor Brown of
the Philadelphia Gazette, Aurora, Aug. 15, 1799. By
"Eliza."   *861.

("Laws are for Sinners"), on injustice under Federalists,
Aurora, Aug. 16, 1799. By "Robert Slender." Leary.
Letters, No. XVIII.   862.

("British Hopes to Regain America"), Aurora, Aug. 17, 1799.

By "Robert Slender." Leary. <u>Letters,</u> No. XV. 863.

("Baking, the New Army Punishment"), satire on military
punishments, <u>Aurora,</u> Aug. 20, 1799. By "Robert
Slender." Leary. <u>Letters,</u> No. XVI. 864.

("Sailors, Avoid the Navy")--on the Jonathan Robbins case--
<u>Aurora,</u> Aug. 20, 1799. By "American Soldier." *865.

("British Interference"), on British minister's remarks,
<u>Aurora,</u> Aug. 23, 1799. By "Robert Slender". Leary.
<u>Letters,</u> No. XVII. 866.

("Jonathan Robbins and British Impressment"), criticism of
Adams, <u>Aurora,</u> Aug. 24, 1799. By "Robert Slender."
Leary. <u>Letters,</u> No. XIX. 867.

("The Sacrifice of Robbins"), with poetic epitaph, <u>Aurora,</u>
Sept. 3, 1799. By "Robert Slender." Leary. <u>Letters,</u>
No. XX. 868.

"Political Reflections"--like an editorial, on admiration for
France, British opposition to democracy and plots against
America--<u>Aurora,</u> Sept. 5, 1799. *869.

("Federalist Mysteries"), <u>Aurora,</u> Sept. 11, 1799. By
"Robert Slender." Leary. <u>Letters,</u> No. XXII. 870.

("Ross, Robbins, and France"), supposed extract of letter,
but probably fiction--<u>Aurora,</u> Sept. 20, 1799. By "P----."
*871.

("McKean, Ross and Selfish Voting"), dialog between Alien and

Citizen--Aurora, Sept. 27, 1799. By "Robert Slender."
Leary. Letters, No. XXIII. 872.

("Ross-McKean Gossip"), humorous, Aurora, Sept. 28, 1799.
Not in the Letters. By "Robert Slender." Leary. 873.

("Vote for McKean and Liberty")--Aurora, Oct. 2, 1799.
Leary. Letters, No. XXIV. (McKean won). 874.

("Robbins's Last Letter"), obvious fiction--Aurora, Oct. 5,
1799. By "Jonathan Robbins." *875.

"Pertinax labor et disciplina omnia vircunt"--proposal to
replace public water with beer--Aurora, Nov. 2, 1799.
By "Timothy Deep." *876.

("The Election--McKean's Merits")--Aurora, Nov. 6, 1799.
By "Robert Slender." Leary. 877.

("Orthodoxy's Inconsistencies"), talk with a preacher--
Aurora, Nov. 9, 1799. By "Robert Slender." Leary.
878.

("My Pleasures in the Army"), ironic, in "Slender" style--
Aurora, Nov. 14, 1799. By "A Refugee." *879.

("Intercepted Letter"), supposed letter by Cramond, English
merchant at Philadelphia, to Parish, American consul at
Hamburg, criticizing American government, with Cramond's
denial in same issue--Aurora, Nov. 23, 1799. By "Robert
Slender." Leary. 880.

("British Secret Service Money")--Aurora, Nov. 30, 1799. By

"Robert Slender." Leary.   881.

("Christianity's Cruelties")--<u>Aurora,</u> Dec. 4, 1799. By
    "Robert Slender." Leary.   882.

("Dangers in Adams's Leadership")--<u>Aurora,</u> Dec. 10, 1799.
    By "Saratoga." Quote from Sterne, and verse.   *883.

<u>Letters on Various interesting and important Subjects...</u>
    By Robert Slender, <u>O. S. M.</u>, Philadelphia, Dec. 30,
    1799. 24 letters and preface; nos. XII (except for poem)
    and XXI did not appear in <u>Aurora;</u> the others did appear--
    March 25, 29, April 23, May 3, 7, 16, 20, June 11, 18,
    19, July 6 (poem only), Aug. 1, 8, 9, 16, 20, 23, 24,
    Sept. 3, 11, 27, Oct. 2, 1799. BAL, Paltsits, Leary.
    Also in facsimile, New York, 1943.

Preface to <u>Letters,</u> on choice of the degree <u>O. S. M.</u>[20](one
    of the swinish multitude), the dedication (to American
    patriots). Not separately noted by Leary. By "Robert
    Slender."   884.

"Letter XII", introduction to poem, "<u>Fourth of July</u>--An Ode,"
    writ supposedly by Slender's neighbor. Not separately
    noted by Leary. By "Robert Slender."   885.

"Letter XXI", on Robbins's citizenship--not from <u>Aurora,</u>[21]
    and not separately noted by Leary. By "Robert Slender."
                                                        886.

1800

("Elegies of Washington"), satire with original verse--<u>Aurora,</u>

130

Jan. 8, 1800. By "Robt. Buckskin," poem signed "Bob
Buckskin."   *887.

("Women to Replace Men?"), satire on adulation of Mrs.
John Adams--Aurora, April 10, 1800. By "Cleopatra."
                                                        *888.

("America's Decline"), talk with immigrant inventor, for
more liberal patent laws--Aurora, April 11, 1800. By
"A Friend to Genius and the Arts."   *889.

("Two Presidents Possible"), satire on Ross bill legalizing
Congress' appointment of President-Aurora, April 14,
1800. By "Francis Foresight."   *890.

("British Impressment of Americans"), nautical and illiterate--
Aurora, May 2, 1800. By "Nathan Cornstalk."   *891.

"To William Duane: Rat Catcher, to their Majesties the
People of the United States", on how to catch Fed rats--
Aurora, July 11, 1800. By "An Old Rat-Catcher, Lately
left off business."   *892.

("Beware, Duane!"), chiding for revealing Fed secrets--
Aurora, Aug. 5, 1800. By "Robert Slender." Leary.
                                                        893.

("Preachers' Worldly Interests"), vs. preaching politics,
especially by Rev. James Abercrombie--Aurora, Sept. 10,
1800. By "Robert Slender." Leary.   894.

("Political Lies"), satire on Feds--Aurora, Oct. 2, 1800.
By "Robert Slender." Leary.   895.

131

"Robert Slender Argueth with the Parson", on preaching
politics--Aurora, Oct. 9, 1800. By "Robert Slender."
Leary. (Oct. 7.)   896.

("The Case against Adams"), opinions of farmers, black-
smiths, doctors, preachers, lawyers, and especially
sailors--Aurora, Oct. 20, 1800. By "The Horse-Doctor."
*897.

("Results of Moving the Government"), on Fed plan of
exclusive rule--Aurora, Nov. 17, 1800. By "Robert
Slender." Leary (Nov. 14).   898.

("Civil War with Jefferson's Election?"), Feds' unfair designs
--Aurora, Nov. 18, 1800. By "Robert Slender." Leary.
899.

1801

("Jefferson and the National Gazette"), defense, reply to
pamphlet renewing Hamilton's 1792 charges--CG, Jan. 5,
1801. By "Philip Freneau." In Aurora, Aug. 14, 1802.
Leary.   900.

("Let Us be Calm"), on tensions as House ballotted for Burr
and Jefferson--Aurora, Feb. 19, 1801. By "Robert
Slender." Leary.   901.

("Slavery to British Fashions")--Aurora, July 2, 1801. By
"Juba."   *902.

("Awarding Offices"), criticism of Henry Miller, Fed replaced
by General Muhlenberg--Tories should be replaced by
Democrats--Aurora, July 8, 1801. By "An Old Soldier."
*903.

("Kittera's Removal"), defending Jefferson--Aurora, Aug. 18,
   1801. By "Menippus."   *904.

The True American, James Wilson,[22] editor-publisher,
   Trenton, N.J. TA.

One of the Swinish Multitude[23] series, vs. Feds: TA, Aug.
   18, Sept. 8, 1801. By "One of the Swinish Multitude."
                                                              *

("Fed Malcontents")--TA, Aug. 18, 1801. By "One of the
   Swinish Multitude."   *905.

("Adams and the Multitude")--TA, Sept. 8, 1801. By "One
   of the Swinish Multitude."   *906.

A Jerseyman series, defense of the Jefferson administration:
   TA, Sept. 29, Oct. 6, 1801; Feb. 23, July 19, 1802;
   Sept. 5, 1803. By "A Jerseyman."   *

("Plots against the Government")--TA, Sept. 29, 1801. By
   "A Jerseyman."   *907.

("Jefferson's Dismissals")--TA, Oct. 6, 1801. By "A Jerseyman."   *908.

("Wrong Republican Innovations"), ironic--Aurora, Dec. 2,
   1801. By "Regiphilus."   *909.

                              1802

"French Spoliations," for paying veterans for ship losses--
   Aurora, Feb. 10, 1802. By "A Merchant and Soldier of
   '76."   *910.

("The Juciary Law Repeal")--TA, Feb. 23, 1802. By "A
  Jerseyman."   *911.

Atticus series, vs. mint, bank, Fed bank monopoly, for
  democratic bank: Aurora, Feb. 11, 16, 23, 24, 1802.
  By "Atticus."   *

("Abolish the Mint")--Aurora, Feb. 11, 1802. By "Atticus."
                                                       *912.

("Mints and Banks Favor Private Interests")--Aurora, Feb.
  16, 1802. By "Atticus."   *913.

("Defense of the West"), reply to Strickland's Observations
  on the Agriculture of the United States--Aurora, Feb. 17,
  1802. By "An American."   *914.

("The Repeal of the Judiciary Act")--TA, Feb. 23, 1802.
  By "A Jerseyman."   *915.

("The Trend of Women's Clothes")--criticism of too little
  clothing--Aurora, Feb. 19, 1802. By "D. K."   *916.

("D. D. K.'s Ignorance"), reply by a woman, supposedly--
  Aurora, Feb. 20, 1802. By "F---- P----," (PF
  reversed?).   *917.

"American Miracle"--comic report of Rembrandt Peale's
  mammoth skeleton and toasts drunk in it--Aurora, Feb.
  22, 1802.   *918.

("Democratic Bank Needed")--Aurora, Feb. 23, 24, 1802.
  By "Atticus."   *919.

134

("Operating the New Bank")--Aurora, March 3, 1802. By "Atticus."
*920.

"Desultory Reflections," retort to article mourning Federalism's passing, criticism of Adams administration--Aurora, March 4, 1802. By "Brimborion."
*921.

Barnaby Bodkin series, on politics: TA, May 11, June 7, 1802. By "Barnaby Bodkin."
*

("On Politics"), dialog in "Slender" style--TA, May 11, 1802. By "Barnaby Bodkin," a tailor.
*922.

("The Political Situation")--TA, June 7, 1802. By "Barnaby Bodkin."
*923.

("A Defense of Burr")--TA, July 19, 1802. By "A Jerseyman."
*924.

"To the Citizens of South Carolina"[24]--from CG, Jan. 5, 1801, q.v.--Aurora, Aug. 11, 1802. By "Philip Freneau." 925.

("Jefferson's Appointments"), defense--Aurora, Aug. 31, 1802. By "Republicanus."
*926.

"Whig and Tory," protest at Feds' attempt to change their name--Aurora, Sept. 18, 1802. By "Bunker-Hill." *927.

("Duane in Danger"), ironic, illiterate satire of Duane's enemies--Aurora, Oct. 6, 1802. By "Herman." *928.

("The Superior Federalists"), ironic praise--Aurora, Nov. 11,

1802.   By "A Federalist."   *929.

<u>1803</u>

("Satire on the Feds")--TA, Jan. 31, 1803, with note signed
   by "One of the Swinish Multitude."   *930.

("Satan and Wilson"), poetic dialog satire--TA, Feb. 28,
   1803, with note signed by "One of the Swinish Multitude."
                                                             *931.

("What is Fun?"), satire on Assembly Speaker Coxe, in
   "Slender" style--TA, April 4, 1803. By "Rigdumfunnidos."
                                                             *932.

"The late attack of Coward & Co. upon Mr. Wilson", on
   beating of Editor Wilson by Wall and Coward--TA, Sept.
   5, 1803. By "A Jerseyman."   *933.

<u>1804</u>
                   25
<u>Bunker</u> series: <u>Aurora</u>, Aug. 25-Oct. 5, 1804, signed "Joe
   Bunker", "Joe Bunker, Jun.", "Jonathan Bunker," and
   "Polly Bunker"--on dispute between <u>Aurora</u> and Tench
   Coxe over Michael Leib and William Penrose, candidates
   for Congress, and a "third party" led by Coxe. <u>Aurora</u>,
   Aug. 25, 28, 29, 30 (two), 31, Sept. 1, 3, 4, 5, (two),
   6, 7, 8, 25, 27 (two), 29, Oct. 4, 5, 1804. All are
   decidedly in the style of "Robert Slender." Leary.

("Duane Wrong to Support Leib"), ironic, satire on Coxe
   and Penrose--<u>Aurora</u>, Aug. 25, 1804. By "Joe Bunker."
                                                             *934.

("Penrose Better Qualified"), ironic, with nautical terms--
   <u>Aurora</u>, Aug. 28, 1804. By "Joe Bunker."   *935.

("Duane's Mistakes"), on the editor's "unprofitable" opposition to Penrose--<u>Aurora</u>, Aug. 29, 1804. By "Joe Bunker, Jun."   *936.

("Coxe's Alleged Faults"), ironic, with verse--<u>Aurora</u>, Aug. 30, 1804. By "Joe Bunker."   *937.

("More Duane Mistakes"), ironic satire of Coxe--<u>Aurora</u>, Aug. 30, 1804. By "Jonathan Bunker," Joe's nephew.
                                                         *938.

("Coxe's Merits"), ironic--<u>Aurora</u>, Aug. 31, 1804. By "Joe Bunker."   *939.

"To Tench Coxe, Esq.", charges of hypocrisy, intrigue, boasts, errors, etc.--<u>Aurora</u>, Aug. 31, 1804. By "Caius Gracchus."   *940.

("T----C----, Spewed from Hell"), like editorial, with verse--<u>Aurora</u>, Sept. 1, 1804.   *941.

("Advice to Duane"), ironic criticism of Democratic Party-- <u>Aurora</u>, Sept. 1, 1804. By "Jonathan Bunker."   *942.

("Defense of Coxe and Objections to Jefferson"), ironic-- <u>Aurora</u>, Sept. 3, 1804. By "Jonathan Bunker."   *943.

("Coxeites' Virtues"), satire--<u>Aurora</u>, Sept. 4, 1804. By "Joe Bunker."   *944.

("Penrose a Genius"), satire in literary and nautical terms --<u>Aurora</u>, Sept. 5, 1804. By "Joe Bunker."   *945.

("Duane, Beware!"),²⁶ mock criticism, satire of Penrose--
   Aurora, Sept. 5, 1804. By "Joe Bunker, Junr."   *946.

("Democratic Tar and Feathers"), mock fears--Aurora,
   Sept. 6, 1804. By "Jonathan Bunker."   *947.

("Duane's Folly in Supporting Leib"), satire on Coxe--
   Aurora, Sept. 7, 1804. By "Joe Bunker."   *948.

("Our Fears of the Democrats"), mock fears--Aurora,
   Sept. 8, 1804. By "Jonathan Bunker."   *949.

("The Bunkers are Right--Praise for Coxe"), ironic--
   Aurora, Sept. 10, 1804. By "Tom Grumbler."   *950.

("The Quids' Oddities"), satire on Coxe and Coxeites--
   Aurora, Sept. 25, 1804. By "Joe Bunker."   *951.

("Leib's Faults--Penrose Perfect"), ironic--Aurora,
   Sept. 27, 1804. By "Joe Bunker."   *952.

("The Duane-Barker Brawl--Plans after Coxe Wins")--
   Aurora, Sept. 27, 1804. By "Jonathan Bunker."   *953.

("Jonathan's Obsession with Politics"), comic--Aurora,
   Sept. 29, 1804. By "Polly Bunker."   *954.

("Coxe's Promises--Signs of Quid Victory")--Aurora,
   Oct. 4, 1804. By "Jonathan Bunker."   *955.

("Jonathan's Neglect of Work")--Aurora, Oct. 5, 1804.
   By "Polly Bunker."   *956.

Tomo Cheeki series, attacks on Coxe--only known use of
pseudonym series since Freneau's in TP, 1797--Aurora,
Oct. 4, 6, 8, 1804. By "Tomo Cheeki." Leary.

("Coxe, Falsifier"), Aurora, Oct. 4, 1804. By "Tomo
Cheeki."   957.

("Coxe's Reply, Mere Repetition")--Aurora, Oct. 6, 1804.
By "Tomo Cheeki."   958.

("Coxe's Attempt to Sell Slaves")--Aurora, Oct. 8, 1804.
By "Tomo Cheeki."   959.

The Duel series,[27] defense of Burr, criticism of Hamilton:
Aurora, Nov. 15, 17, 21, 26, 1804. By "Sylvius, "
Freneau pseudonym.

"The Duel, " No. I, introduction, on Hamilton's opposition
to the Constitution in 1787--Aurora, Nov. 15, 1804.
By "Sylvius, " Freneau pseudonym.   960.

"The Duel, " No. II, on Hamilton's evasions to Burr--
Aurora, Nov. 17, 1804. By "Sylvius, " Freneau
pseudonym.   961.

"The Duel, " No. III, on Hamilton's secretive last words--
Aurora, Nov. 21, 1804. By "Sylvius, " Freneau
pseudonym.   962.

"The Duel, " No. IV, on Morris's eulogy of Hamilton, dangers
of adulation, with Shakespeare quote--Aurora, Nov. 26,
1804. By "Sylvius, " Freneau pseudonym.   963.

139

Secundum Quid-Tertium Quid series,[28] vs. McKean and his
 party: Aurora, June 4, 12, 18, 26, 1805. By "Secundum Quid" and "Tertium Quid."   *

("McKean and his Constitutionalists"), satire in "Slender"
 style--Aurora, June 4, 1805. By "Secundum Quid." *964.

("Should I Join the Constitutionalists?"), satire--Aurora,
 June 12, 1805. By "Secundum Quid."   *965.

("Lawyers are Like Hornets"), satire on McKean party--
 Aurora, June 18, 1805. By "Tertium Quid," formerly
 "Secundum Quid."   *966.

("Inside the McKean Party"), satire by a new member--
 Aurora, June 26, 1805. By "A Tertium Quid."   *967.

("McKean an Aristocrat")--Aurora, June 22, 1805. By
 "Philocles."   *968.

Bobby Tipstaff series, vs. McKean: Aurora, Sept. 5, 12,
 1805. By "Bobby Tipstaff."   *

("A McKean Constable's Job"), satire in "Slender" style,
 of McKean politics, by a summons server--Aurora,
 Sept. 5, 1805. By "Bobby Tipstaff."   *969.

("Fears of a McKean Election"), mock fears--Aurora,
 Sept. 12, 1805. By "Bobby Tipstaff."   *970.

("A Conversion to Snyder"), tale in "Slender" style, of Tipstaff's grandma's desertion of McKean--<u>Aurora,</u> Sept. 25, 1805. By "Thomas Doubtful." (McKean won.)   *971.

1806

"His Majesty, and the Turnpike Gate!"--satire on English king, forced to pay one-cent toll--<u>Aurora,</u> Sept. 1, 1806. By "A Supporter of Royalty."   *972.

("Donaldson's Merits"), ironic (D. was candidate for sheriff) --<u>Aurora,</u> Sept. 29, 1806. By "A Staunch Quid." *973.

1807

("General Barker's Orders"), satire on the military sheriff, in "Slender" style--<u>Aurora,</u> Aug. 6, 1807. By "Fudge."
*974.

1808

<u>Juba</u> series, for Jefferson: <u>Aurora,</u> [29] July 13, 20, 1808. By "Juba."

"Serious Reflections," defense of Jefferson's administration --<u>Aurora,</u> July 13, 1808. By "Juba."   *975.

("Jefferson and the Federalist Record")--<u>Aurora,</u> July 20, 1808. By "Juba."   *976.

("The Bad Adams Administration")--<u>Aurora,</u> Aug. 12, 1808. By "Yorick."   *977.

("The Philadelphia Academy Commencement"), ridicule of "Dr. A."--<u>Aurora,</u> Aug. 4, 1808. By "A. B.", Freneau pseudonym.   978.

("The Federalist Attitude"), ironic defense--<u>Aurora,</u> Aug. 18, 1808. By "A Staunch Federalist." *979.

<u>Juba</u> Series, attacks on James Ross, candidate for governor: <u>Aurora,</u> Aug. 22, 30, Sept. 10, 1808. By "Juba." *

("Ross's Faults")--<u>Aurora,</u> Aug. 22, 1808. By "Juba." *980.

("Ross and Mrs. Marie"), --on Ross's ejection of a Mrs. Marie from her home, Grant's Hill in Pittsburgh, which he had partly bought from her husband--<u>Aurora,</u> Aug. 24, 1808. By "Grant's Hill." *981.

("Cobbett and British History"), satire--<u>Aurora,</u> Aug. 26, 1808. By "Tisiphone." Reprinted, <u>Aurora,</u> Nov. 23, 1808. *982.

("The Resolutions for Ross"), satire--<u>Aurora,</u> Aug. 30, 1808. By "Juba." *983.

("Ross and Snyder"), vs. Ross--<u>Aurora,</u> Sept. 10, 1808. By "Juba." *984.

("Embargo Benefits")--writer calls self a ship-master-- <u>Aurora,</u> Nov. 17, 1808. By "Nauticus." *985.

<u>Old Soldier</u> series, vs. King George and Britain: <u>Aurora,</u> Nov. 19, 21, Dec. 15, 29, 30, 1808; March 22, 1809. By "Old Soldier." *

("George III, Tyrant")--<u>Aurora,</u> Nov. 19, 1808. By "An Old Soldier." *986.

("Federalist Cooperation with King George")--<u>Aurora,</u> Nov. 21, 1808. By "The Old Soldier." *987.

("Declare War on England")--<u>Aurora,</u> Dec. 15, 1808. By "The Old Soldier." *988.

"'Facts are Stubborn Things,' and not the less so for being in a plain and simple dress", on Tory plot to divide Union--<u>Aurora,</u> Dec. 26, 1808. By "Gates." *989.

("Attack Canada")--<u>Aurora,</u> Dec. 29, 1808. By "The Old Soldier." *990.

("Half-Pay Pensions for Veterans")--<u>Aurora,</u> Dec. 30, 1808. By "The Old Soldier." *991.

<u>1809</u>

("Tory Devotion to Britain")--<u>Aurora,</u> Jan. 10, 1809. By "Warren." *992.

<u>The American</u> series, defense of Jefferson administration: <u>Aurora,</u> Jan. 24, Feb. 1, 8, 1809. Titled "The American." *

("Federalists Obstruct the Government")--<u>Aurora,</u> Jan. 24, 1809. Titled "The American-No. I." *993.

("Let Us Have Harmony"), defense of Embargo--<u>Aurora,</u> Jan. 31, 1809. By "Timon." *994.

("Jefferson and the Embargo")--<u>Aurora,</u> Feb. 1, 1809. Titled "The American--No. II." *995.

("The American British Faction")--<u>Aurora</u>, Feb. 8, 1809.
Titled "The American--No. III."   *996.

A <u>Federalist</u> series, vs. Britain, for Embargo: <u>Aurora</u>,
Feb. 13, 15, 1809. By "A Federalist."   *

("Keep the Embargo")--<u>Aurora</u>, Feb. 13, 1809. By "A
Federalist."   *997.

("Embargo, Means for Peace")--<u>Aurora</u>, Feb. 15, 1809.
By "A Federalist."   *998.

("Britain's Faults"), satire in "Slender" style--<u>Aurora</u>, Feb.
22, 1809. By "G.", Freneau pseudonym.   999.

("War with Britain Inevitable")--<u>Aurora</u>, March 22, 1809.
By "The Old Soldier."   *1000.

("Gideon Olmsted"), defense of veteran who lost ship and
claimed reimbursement, with Shakespeare quote--<u>Aurora</u>,
April 19, 1809. By "Old Continental Currency."   *1001.

("Watch England!")--<u>Aurora</u>, April 21, 1809. By "<u>A Man
of 1775</u>."   *1002.

<u>Chares</u> series, vs. Britain--<u>Aurora</u>, June 22, 23, 24, 26,
27, 1809. By "Chares."   *

("British Bad Faith"), historical review, with evident know-
ledge of shipping--<u>Aurora</u>, June 22, 1809. By "Chares."
                                                       *1003.

("England and France"), historical comparison, vs. England--

<u>Aurora,</u> June 23, 1809. By "Chares." *1004.

("American English Relations"), historical review, emphasizing <u>Chesapeake</u> affair--- <u>Aurora,</u> June 24, 1809. By
"Chares." *1005.

("Embargo is a Success")--<u>Aurora,</u> June 26, 1809. By
"Chares." *1006.

("British Desperation")--<u>Aurora,</u> June 27, 1809. By "Chares."
*1007.

<u>A Democrat</u> series, vs. Federalists and England--<u>Aurora,</u>
July 1, Aug. 18, 25, 29, Sept. 16, 1809. By "A
Democrat." *

("Democrats and Federalists"), advice to Feds to change
name--<u>Aurora,</u> July 1, 1809. By "A Democrat." *1008.

<u>Mentor</u> series: <u>Aurora,</u> July 26, Aug. 1, 21, Nov. 28,
Dec. 12, 1809. By "Mentor." *

(" Our Exhausted Commerce"), retort to Timothy Pickering--
<u>Aurora,</u> July 26, 1809. By "A Mentor." *1009.

("Embargo, Only Way Out of War"), on need of reviving
embargo, now repealed--<u>Aurora,</u> Aug. 1, 1809. By
"Mentor." *1010.

("British Perfidy")--<u>Aurora,</u> Aug. 18, 1809. Titled "The
Democrat" and unsigned. *1011.

("Britain Will Not Change")--<u>Aurora,</u> Aug. 21, 1809.By "Mentor."
*1012.

("Causes of Party Dissensions")--Aurora, Aug. 25, 1809.
   Titled "The Democrat" and unsigned.   *1013.

("Jefferson's Wisdon")--Aurora, Aug. 29, 1809. Titled
   "The Democrat."   *1014.

("Britain's Commercial Rulers")--Aurora, Sept. 16, 1809.
   By "The Democrat."   *1015.

An American series, "To the Federalists"- Aurora, Sept. 27,
   28, 1809. By "An American."   *

("Defense of Madison")--Aurora, Sept. 27, 1809. By "An
   American."   *1016.

("Support Madison")--Aurora, Sept. 28, 1809. By "An
   American."   *1017.

("Feds Still Pro-British"), dialog between "Whig" and "Fed"
   --Aurora, Oct. 2, 1809. By "Caution."   *1018.

An Old Soldier series, to the Whigs: Aurora, Oct, 7, 9, 10,
   1809. By "An Old Soldier."   *

"To the Whigs", that Whigs are better than Feds--Aurora,
   Oct. 7, 1809. By "An Old Soldier."   *1019.

("For Madison, Free Trade, and No Tribute"), Aurora,
   Oct. 9, 1809. By "An Old Soldier."   *1020

("Let All Vote")--Aurora, Oct. 10, 1809. By "An Old
   Soldier."   *1021.

146

("New Weekly, The Hemisphere"), criticism, and defense of
Napoleon--Aurora, Oct. 19, 1809. By "An American."
*1022.

("Manufacturing is Needed")--Aurora, Oct. 25, 1809. By
"N.", Freneau pseudonym.   1023.

("War is Abominable")--Aurora, Nov. 13, 1809. By "Nathan'
--in the style of "Slender."   *1024.

Mentor series, to Congress: Aurora, Nov. 28, Dec. 12,
1809. By "Mentor."   *

("Better to Fight England than France")--Aurora, Nov. 28,
1809. By "Mentor."   *1025.

("Britain's Weaknesses"), on capture of Canada--Aurora,
Dec. 12, 1809. By "Mentor."   *1026.

("Feds' Blindness to Jackson's Conduct"), criticism of
British minister, with allegory on British-American
relations- Aurora, Dec. 22, 1809. By "Oh Times!
Oh Manners!"   *1027.

1810

("The British Minister")--Aurora, Jan. 1, 1810. By "An
American."   *1028.

Stophel Funk series, in "Slender" manner, vs. Gov. Snyder:
Aurora, Jan. 20, 25, 27, Feb. 1, 6, 8, 15, 1810. By
"Stophel Funk."   *

("Snyder, Governor Extraordinary"), ironic, with Hudibras

147

quote--Aurora, Jan. 20, 1810. By "Stophel Funk." *1029.

("Weiser's Bias"), reply to critic of Snyder, "Conrad
Weiser," ironic--Aurora, Jan. 25, 1810. By "Stophel
Funk." *1030.

("Snyder's Address"), ironic praise, reference to "Robert
Slender" ^{30}Aurora, Jan. 27, 1810. By "Stophel Funk."
*1031.

("General Bright and the State Constitution")--satire--Aurora,
Feb. 1, 1810. By "Stophel Funk." *1032.

("The Governor's Speech"), ironic praise in oration form--
Aurora, Feb. 6, 1810. By "Stophel Funk." *1033.

("Snyder and Bright and the U. S. Constitution"), satire in
oration form--Aurora, Feb. 8, 1810. By "Stophel Funk."
*1034.

("Snyder's Letter to Madison"), satire with verse--Aurora,
Feb. 15, 1810. By "Stophel Funk." *1035.

("The Opposition to Torpedoes"), satire on Representatives
Dana, Quincy, and others--Aurora, March 16, 1810.
By "Apuletus's Ass." *1036.

("The United States Bank Charter"), against renewal--
Aurora, Nov. 29, 1810. By "The Old Soldier." *1037.

1811

The Bank Distemper series: Aurora, Jan. 18, 22, 28, Feb.
14, 23, 1811. By "Sangrado." *

"The Bank Distemper!!" No. I--satire on the U. S. Bank
and Mathew Carey in "Slender" style--Aurora, Jan. 18,
1811. By "Sangrado."   *1038.

"The Bank Distemper!!" No. II--more satire on Carey, who
is described as in a furious temper--Aurora, Jan. 22,
1811. By "Sangrado."   *1039.

"The Bank Distemper!!" No. III--Carey at the Coffee House
--Aurora, Jan. 28, 1811. By "Sangrado."   *1040.

"The Bank Distemper!!" No. IV, mock-medical discussion of
of "bank fever," with reference to Carey's pamphlet on
the 1793 yellow fever epidemic--Aurora, Feb. 14, 1811.
By "Sangrado."   *1041.

"The Bank Distemper!!" No. V, mock-medical discussion of
insanity, implying that Carey is a victim--Aurora, Feb.
23, 1811. By "Sangrado."   *1042.

Indian Affairs series: Aurora, Dec. 12, 19, 20, 30, 1811;
Jan. 1, 18, 1812. By "An Old Soldier."   *

"Indian Affairs" No. II, on origin of Shawanese Indians--
Aurora, Dec. 12, 1811. By "An Old Soldier."   *1043.

"Indian Affairs" No. III, on absence of tribal boundaries--
Aurora, Dec. 19, 1811. By "An Old Soldier."   *1044.

"Indian Affairs" No. I, on tour of Indian lands--Aurora,
Dec. 20, 1811. By "An Old Soldier."   *1045.

"Indian Affairs" No. IV, on the Indian war and practical
measures--Aurora, Dec. 30, 1811. By "An Old Soldier."
*1046.

1812

"Indian Affairs" No. V, on John Randolph's speeches, defense
of Wayne--Aurora, Jan. 1, 1812. By "An Old Soldier."
*1047.

"Indian Affairs" No. VI, on speeches of Randolph, "that
mongrel Indian"--Aurora, Jan. 18, 1812. By "An Old
Soldier."   *1048.

Old Soldier essays[32] on various topics: Aurora, Oct. 21, Nov.
14, 24, Dec. 9, 14, 23, 1812; Jan. 15, Feb. 5, June 2,
Dec. 29, 1813; Jan. 10, Aug. 11, Sept. 8, Nov. 10, 14,
19, 22, 23, 26, 28, 1814; Jan. 2, 13, Feb. 2, 3, March
30, July 10, Aug. 25, 1815. By the "Old Soldier."   *

("Report from the West"), vs. Tories and British--Aurora,
Oct. 21, 1812. By "The Old Soldier."   *1049.

"The Old Indian School Must Be Changed", on unwisdom
of leniency--Aurora, Nov. 14, 1812. By "The Old
Soldier."   *1050.

"The old Indian School must be abandoned", defense of our
treatment of Indians now--Aurora, Nov. 24, 1812. By
"The Old Soldier."   *1051.

"The Old Indian School Must End", on Indian conditions in
Ohio--Aurora, Dec. 9, 1812. By "The Old Soldier."
*1052.

("Take Halifax"), on need of strong navy--Aurora, Dec. 11,

150

1812.   By "An Old Soldier."   *1053.

"The Old Indian System Must Be Changed, " on right of
   conquest--Aurora, Dec. 14, 1812.   By "The Old Soldier."
                                                           *1054.

The Navy series: Aurora, Dec. 22, 24, 1812.   By "Hawser
   Trunnion, "[33] Freneau pseudonym.

("Need of Larger Navy")--Aurora, Dec. 22, 1812.   By
   "Hawser Trunnion, " Freneau pseudonym.   Leary.   1055.

("Planned Preparation"), on expected Indian war--Aurora,
   Dec. 23, 1812.   By "The Old Soldier."   *1056.

"The Navy--II", on folly of rivalling British Navy--Aurora,
   Dec. 24, 1812.   By "Hawser Trunnion, " Freneau
   pseudonym.   1057.

1813

("Need of Cavalry")--Aurora, Jan. 15, 1813.   By "The Old
   Soldier."   *1058.

("Infantry Methods")--Aurora, Feb. 5, 1813.   By "The Old
   Soldier."   *1059.

("Long Speeches in Congress"), criticism--Aurora, Feb. 6,
   1813.   By "Semper Eadem."   *1060.

L. Series: Aurora, April 30, June 1, July 3 (two), 1813.
   By "L."   *

("Ignorant Castlereagh"), criticism of English premier--

Aurora, April 30, 1813. By "L."   *1061.

("The Essex Submissioners"), vs. New England leaders--
    Aurora, June 1, 1813. By "L."   *1062.

("The Army at Work"), on error about General Pike--Aurora,
    June 2, 1813. By "An Old Soldier."   *1063.

(Naval Delays")--Aurora, July 3, 1813. By "L."   *1064.

"Internal Navigation"--Aurora, July 3, 1813. By "L."*1065.

("Mourning for General Kutusoff"), satire on Benevolent
    Society of Cossacks--Aurora, July 19, 1813. Signed
    "Broadbrim, Sharpshins, Secretaries."   *1066.

("Dilatory Congress")--Aurora, July 20, 1813. By
    "Agricola."   *1067.

("Navy Heroes Not Feds")--Aurora, Sept. 30, 1813. By
    "An American."   *1068.

"Eastern Patriotism", criticism of New England, quotes
    from Graydon's Memoirs--Aurora, Oct. 7, 1813. By
    "Seventy-Six."   *1069.

Americus series: Aurora, Oct. 20, 26, Nov. 6, 1813. By
    "Americus."   *

("Our Pessimists")--Aurora, Oct. 20, 1813. By "Americus."
                                                   *1070.
The Fredonian, D. and J. Fitz Randolph, publishers, New
    Brunswick, N. J.

("Republican Management of the Navy"), defense--Fredonian,
Oct. 21, 1813. By "A Friend to the Navy."   *1071.

("Federalist Editors Love the English")--Aurora, Oct. 26,
1813. By "Americus."   *1072.

("Federalists' Failure to Support the War")--Aurora, Oct.
26, 1813. By "Americus."   *1073.

("The Sentiment against American Victories")[35]--Aurora,
Nov. 6, 1813. By "Atticus."   *1074.

Agricola series, mostly on naval problems: Aurora, Nov. 10,
Dec. 16, 17, 29 1813. By "Agricola."   *

("Fighting the English Navy")--Aurora, Nov. 10, 1813. By
"Agricola."   *1075.

("American Prisoners")--Aurora, Dec. 10, 1813. By
"Hornet."   *1076.

"On Our means of Injuring the Commerce of the Enemy,"
for bigger navy now--Aurora, Dec. 16, 1813. By
"Agricola."   *1077.

("Our Navy"), cont. of 1075--Aurora, Dec. 17, 1813. By
"Agricola."   *1078.

("The Veterans' Sufferings")--Aurora, Dec. 29, 1813. By
"The Old Soldier."   *1079.

("British Prisons")--Aurora, Dec. 29, 1813. By "Agricola."
                                                   *1080.

"Remarks on the Address of the Kentuckian", on Indians'
lack of property rights--Aurora, Jan. 10, 1814. By
"The Old Soldier."   *1081.

The New-York Weekly Museum, or Ladies' Weekly Museum,
James Oram, editor-publisher, New York. WM.

("Mental Cultivation in Women")--WM, March 5, 1815.
By "F.", Freneau pseudonym.   1082.

("Better Militia Officers")--Aurora, Aug. 11, 1814. By
"An Old Soldier."   *1083.

("Federalist Narrowness")--Aurora, Aug. 23, 1814, dialog
between "Morris" and "Quincy." By "Lucian."   *1084.

("Choose Conferees from Officials"),[36] ironic--Aurora, Aug.
25, 1814. By "Robert Slender," last known appearance.
Leary. (Aug. 11).   1085.

("Praise for Governor Snyder"), ironic--Aurora, Aug. 26,
1814. By "Shamokin, " with reference to "Robert Slender."
                                                           *1086.

("The Pennsylvania Militia"), criticism--Aurora, Sept. 8,
1814. By "An Old Soldier."   *1087.

("The Fall of Washington City"), lament--Aurora, Sept. 9,
1814. By "Tell."   *1088.

"The British Vandals"--Aurora, Oct. 3, 1814. By "L."
                                                           *1089.

("The House's Long Speeches")--<u>Aurora</u>, Nov. 8, 1814.
By "Polymnia."   *1090.

("The New England Faction")--<u>Aurora</u>, Nov. 10, 1814. By
"An Old Soldier."   *1091.

("America's Decay in New England")--<u>Aurora</u>, Nov. 14,
1814. By "An Old Soldier."   *1092.

<u>Olive Branch</u> series, review of Carey's <u>Olive Branch</u>:
<u>Aurora</u>, Nov. 19, 22, 24, 25, 26, 1814. By "An Old
Soldier."   *

("The <u>Olive Branch's</u> Opportune Appearance") --<u>Aurora</u>,
Nov. 19, 1814. By "An Old Soldier."   *1093.

("Jefferson's Administration and <u>The Olive Branch</u>")--<u>Aurora</u>,
Nov. 22, 1814. By "An Old Soldier."   *1094.

("Madison's Administration and <u>The Olive Branch</u>")--<u>Aurora</u>,
Nov. 24, 1814. By "An Old Soldier."   *1095.

("New England, Boston, and <u>The Olive Branch</u>")--<u>Aurora</u>,
Nov. 25, 1814. By "An Old Soldier."   *1096.

("New England's Unfortunate Attitude")--<u>Aurora</u>, Nov. 26,
1814. By "An Old Soldier."   *1097.

("The Ideal National Bank"), to Congress--<u>Aurora</u>, Nov. 28,
1814. By "The Old Soldier."   *1098.

("A Bank for the Yeomanry")--<u>Aurora</u>, Dec. 15, 1814. By

"An Old Soldier."   *1099.

1815

Remarks on the Sine Qua Non series, on wars, money,
    British treachery, Indians, land: Aurora, Jan. 2, 11, 15,
    1815. By "The Old Soldier."   *

"Remarks on the Sine Qua Non" No. I- on war's lessons,
    its need of money--Aurora, Jan. 2, 1815. By "The Old
    Soldier."   *1100.

"Remarks on the Sine Qua Non" No. II, on the Jay Treaty,
    and Wayne's with the Indians--Aurora, Jan. 11, 1815.
    By "The Old Soldier."   *1101.

"Remarks on the Sine Qua Non" No. III, on Indians' lack of
    right to land but by civil compact--Aurora, Jan. 15,
    1815. By "The Old Soldier."   *1102.

("Drive the English Out"), to Congress--Aurora, Feb. 2,
    1815. By "An Old Soldier."   *1103.

("Our Lazy Legislature"), to the state legislators--Aurora,
    Feb. 3, 1815. By "An Old Soldier."   *1104.

("The British and the Indians"), on problem of policy--
    Aurora, March 30, 1815. By "The Old Soldier."   *1105.

("Pro-British Americans")--Aurora, July 10, 1815. By "The
    Old Soldier."   *1106.

"The Subject of a Review of War", justification of war,
    criticism of non-supporters--Aurora, Aug. 25, 1815. By

156

"An Old Soldier."   *1107.

("Printers' Problems"), defense of Aurora in "Slender"
    style--Aurora, Oct. 9, 1815. By "Shamokin."   *1108.

("The Importance of Voting"), to voters--Aurora, Oct. 10,
    1815. By "Scaevola."   *1109.

Codrus series, on government and politics: Aurora, Oct. 13,
    16, 18, 25, 1815. By "Codrus."   *

("Party Names")--Aurora, Oct. 13, 1815. By "Codrus."
                                                         *1110.

("Why Parties?")--Aurora, Oct. 16, 1815. By "Codrus."
                                                         *1111.

("Elections' Manipulations")--Aurora, Oct. 18, 1815. By
    "Codrus."   *1112.

("Parties, Sport for the Few")--Aurora, Oct. 25, 1815.
    By "Codrus."   *1113.

("The Easy Graduation of Doctors"), satire on a Rutgers
    graduation, largely in dialog--Aurora, Nov. 2, 1815.
    By "A Traveller," Freneau pseudonym.   *1114.

1816

Old Soldier series on bank, Treasury, Gallatin, etc.:
    Aurora, Jan. 5, 10, 11, 1816. By "The Old Soldier." *

("Open the Treasury to the Public")--Aurora, Jan. 5, 1816.
    By "The Old Soldier."   *1115.

157

("Duane's Abuse of Dallas"), ironic, in "Slender" style, with lines from Pope and Hamlet--Aurora, Jan. 8, 1816. By "Matthew Ward." *1116.

("Gallatin's Artifices")--Aurora, Jan. 10, 1816. By "The Old Soldier." *1117.

("A National Bank for All the People")--Aurora, Jan. 11, 1816. By "The Old Soldier." *1118.

"Lycidas," a biography--WM, March 23, 1816. By "F.", Freneau pseudonym. 1119.

"Solar Spots," with Horace quote--Aurora, June 21, 1816. By "Z.", Freneau pseudonym. See WM, Sept. 7, 1816. 1120.

"On the Spots in the Sun," with quotes from Hamlet and Julius Ceasar--WM, Sept. 7, 1816. By "P. F." Leary. 1121.

<u>1817</u>

("Carey's Inconsistency"), satire on caucuses--Aurora, June 18, 1817. By "Circumbendibus." *1122.

("Defense of Hiester"), with praise of Joseph Reed-Aurora, July 18, 1817. By "An Old Soldier." *1123.

"The River of Life," dream essay--WM, Sept. 20, 1817. By "L."[37] *1124.

("Findlay, Greatest Whig"), ironic "Slender" style--Aurora, Sept. 23, 1817. By "Stench Coaxe." *1125.

("Patriotic Political Ambitions"), satire on politicians--
   Aurora, Aug. 26, 1818. By "Momus."   *1126.

1820

An Old Soldier series,[38] for Hiester vs. Findlay for governor:
   Aurora, July 11, 20, Aug. 9, 24, 1820. By "An Old
   Soldier."   *

("Findlay's Corrupt Administration")--Aurora, July 11, 1820.
   By "An Old Soldier."   *1127.

"The Contrast," New York under De Witt Clinton and Pennsylvania under Findlay--Aurora, July 20, 1820. By "An
   Old Soldier."   *1128.

("Philadelphia's Decay, Need of Wise Government")--Aurora,
   Aug. 9, 1820. By "An Old Soldier."   *1129.

("Findlay and Hiester"),[39] appeal for votes for Hiester--
   Aurora, Aug. 24, 1820. By "An Old Soldier." (Hiester
   won.)   *1130.

("The Reign of Terror Again?"), mock fears of Adams-type
   rigors, from postmaster's refusal to distribute Aurora--
   in "Slender" style, with apparent reference to Bunker
   Letters of 1804--Aurora, Dec. 5, 1820. By "Joel Bunker,
   Jun. Son of Old Joe."   *1131.

1821

"Office Hunting--a Dream", in "Slender" style, satire on

selfish office seekers--<u>Aurora</u>, Feb. 20, 1821. By
"Somnus." *1132.

"John Q. Adams' Address," in "Slender" style, criticism
of Adams's hypocrisy under ironic praise--<u>Aurora</u>, Aug.
30, 1821. By "Joe Bunker," closing with "I am, Mr.
Duane, your old friend." See Bunker <u>Letters</u> of 1804.
1133.

<u>1822</u>

("Princeton's Need for Help"), appeal to legislature--TA,
Feb. 16, 1822. By "L." *1134.

("On the Moon"), footnote to probable Freneau poem, "The
Female Astronomer"--TA, June 29, 1822. *1135.

<u>Recollections of Past Times and Events</u> series, evidently by
Freneau, signed with letters from his surname--TA,
July 6, 27, Aug. 10, 17, 1822. Leary.

"1. Recollections of past Times and Events", problems
of the Continental currency, tale in dialog--TA, July 6,
1822. By "R." Leary. 1136.

("A Bahama Cave"), poem's introduction, eleboration of essay
in USM, June, 1779. TA, July 13, 1822. 1137.

("General Denouette"), introduction to Freneau poem, "General Lefevre Denouette"--TA, July 20, 1822. Poem signed
"R." Leary notes the poem. 1138.

"2. Recollections of Past Times and Events," on tea
embargo, with poem--TA, July 27, 1822. Poem signed

"U." Leary. 1139.

"3. Recollections of Past Times and Events," on Bermuda,
with poem--TA, Aug. 10, 1822. Poem signed "F."
Leary. 1140.

"4. Recollections of Past Times and Events," subtitled
"Liberty Poles", with poem, "The New Liberty Pole. --
Take Care!"--TA, Aug. 17, 1822. Poem signed "R."
Leary. 1141.

"Historical Memoirs of Past Times", [40] on Columbus's grave
in Domingo--TA, Aug. 17, 1822. Unsigned, but just
above "Recollections" No. 4 and evidently with it. 1142.

1823

"A Vision," dream-essay satire on Shulze, candidate for
governor--Aurora, Oct. 3, 1823. By "Somnus." *1143.

"Election," appeal for votes for Gregg, governor candidate
vs. Shulze--Aurora, Oct. 13, 1823. By "Obadiah."
(Shulze won.) *1144.

1824

"La Fayette," review of Memoirs of Gilbert Motier La
Fayette, by H. L. Holstein, also of Biographie des
Hommes Civants' article, "Marie, Paul, Joseph, Roch,
Ives, Gilbert, Mottiers de la Fayette,"on errors--Aurora,
Sept. 15, 1824. By "K.", Freneau pseudonym. 1145.

1855

"Philip Freneau," Cyclopaedia of American Literature, Evert

161

and George Duyckinck (New York, 1855), I, 328-348--
includes "Advice to Authors" and "Directions for Court-
ship" from MW, only known republication of Freneau's
prose in nineteenth century, after his death.   1146.

1899

Some Account of the Capture of the Ship "Aurora", Jay
Milles, ed., New York, 1899. From 1780 ms. BAL,
Paltsits, Leary.   1147.

1902

The Spy (a third in prose), The Poems of Philip Freneau,
Fred L. Pattee, ed., Princeton, 1902-1907, 3 vols.,
II, 39-72. "Life of Philip Freneau," I, xiii-cxii, has
essays, letters, prose parts.   1148.

1918

Unpublished Freneauana, Charles F. Heartman, ed., New
York, 1918. Has two Freneau letters of 1815 (wrongly
dated 1819) and 1822, to Dr. John Francis, and 1822
proposal for an edition of "Poems and Miscellanies,"
never published.   1149.

1936

"Freneau and Jefferson," by P. M. Marsh, American
Literature, May, 1936. Contains Freneau's defense of
himself and Jefferson, from Aurora, Aug. 11, 1802.
                                                       1150.

1942

"Father Bombo's Pilgrimage," by Lewis Leary, Pennsylvania

162

Magazine, Oct. 1942. Contains Freneau's part of "novel"
writ with Brackenridge at Princeton in 1770, q.v.

1151.

1943

Letters on Various interesting and Important Subjects...
by Robert Slender, H. H. Clark, ed., New York, 1943.
Facsimile of 1799. BAL.

1152.

1955

The Prose of Philip Freneau, Philip M. Marsh, ed., New
Brunswick, N.J., 1955. About 170 selected items.
BAL.

1153.

Notes

1. Parentheses around a title mean that the original had
   no title, and that one has been supplied, based on
   content.

2. Freneau's poems appeared in FJ from February to
   October, 1787.

3. "L." was used often with essays probably by Freneau.
   Addison also used the pseudonym frequently. Leary
   (pp. 211-212) credits this item to Freneau.

4. Brackenridge was in Philadelphia that year; he now
   published the first Modern Chivalry here, and wrote
   several items for the newspapers. See Modern
   Chivalry, Claude M. Newlin, ed., New York, 1937,
   p. xxiv; and P.M. Marsh, "Hugh Henry Brackenridge: More Essays in the National Gazette," Western
   Pennsylvania Historical Magazine, Sept.-Dec., 1946,
   and another, ibid., March, 1954. The writer of the
   first essay says he is "personally unknown" to
   Jefferson, so might well be Brackenridge.

5. Leary (page 218, note 93) recognizes this item as by
   Freneau.

6. A character in Don Quixote, the supposed author of the
   ms. on which Cervantes based the novel.

7. This essay evidently roused Washington's wrath. Jefferson's _Anas_ on May 23 records that, in a talk with Jefferson, the President "adverted to a piece in Freneau's paper of yesterday" and apparently wanted Jefferson to discharge Freneau from the translatorship. Jefferson added, "But I will not do it. His paper has saved our Constitution, which was galloping fast into monarchy, and has been checked by no one means so powerfully as by that paper." An interesting question--did the National Gazette save the United States from monarchy?

8. Freneau wrote a poem, "The Almanac Maker," describing how the almanac maker travels, mentally, among the stars. MW, pages 150-152.

9. The many Freneauesque items in the _Aurora_ now suggest that Freneau was in the city, possibly working for Duane.

10. The continuation of "Freneau" items in the _Aurora_ after he began the Jersey Chronicle suggests that he made weekly or bi-weekly trips to Philadelphia, to buy supplies, talk shop, etc.

11. This is an unwarrantable liberty to take with a republished essay--except where the editor happens to have been the author also--therefore it is excellent evidence, almost proof, that Freneau was in fact none other than the "Old Soldier" himself.

12. More evidence that Freneau was the "Old Soldier."

13. See Freneau's poem, "The Country Printer," which also uses the same central character, "Type."

14. A pseudonym used frequently by Freneau in his 1809 _Poems_.

15. Freneau, who had left New York for Charleston in January, returned on March 14, 1798. See Leary, page 300.

16. Freneau's poem, "To an Alien," appeared in TP, July 13, 1798. Leary, page 469.

17. Thomas Holcroft, English writer, was a friend of Godwin and Paine. The novel _Hugh Trevor_ defended social revolution.

18. After John Fenno's death, September, 1798, GUS was run by his son, John Ward Fenno. On March 2, 1799, he sadly announced its abandonment, though

planning to continue till paid subscriptions were fulfilled.

19. A facsimile edition (New York, 1943), ed. by H. H. Clark, biblio. note, page vi, lists No. XXI from the Aurora of Sept. 28, 1799. But the Sept. 28 essay is not in the Letters, and No. XXI is new.

20. "O. S. M."--Edmund Burke, in Reflections on the Revolution in France, said, "Learning will be cast into the mire, and trodden under the hoofs of a swinish multitude." This aroused many retorts.

21. A new essay. H. H. Clark, editing the facsimile edition of Letters (New York, 1943), p. vi, says it was in Aurora of Sept. 28, 1799. This is not true; the Sept. 28 essay is not in the Letters; Clark must not have examined it.

22. Wilson joined Day and Mann on June 23, 1801, became sole owner in 1804, was pro-Jefferson, anti-Federalist. In the 1801 winter, Freneau returned to Mount Pleasant, and wrote poems for the New York Weekly Museum. It was a lively time for TA till 1803, when he went to sea again.

23. In the Slender Letters, "O. S. M." is used after the "author's" name, meaning "One of the Swinish Multitude." Freneau wrote the last of the series for the Aurora of Feb. 19, 1801.

24. The reprinting of this defense of Jefferson and Freneau, originally published to meet a revival of Hamilton's 1792 charges, in the 1800-1801 presidential campaign, suggests that the charges were still alive in mid-1802, and that Freneau was in Philadelphia, ready to revive his defense of nineteen months before.

25. In Freneau's ms. record of voyages (at MHA), he noted that he returned to Charleston, S. C., from Madeira and Teneriffe, on June 10, 1804. He probably arrived at home in New Jersey shortly thereafter, and thence gravitated to his favorite political arena, Philadelphia.

26. A suspicion that the Bunker letters were by Freneau was current; an evasive reply to the charge appeared in the Aurora, Sept. 5, 1804--"Poor Robert Slender ...his poor head has surely enough to bear without being burthened with the sins of the Bunkers."

27. That Freneau was not in the city is suggested by an

editorial slap in the United States Gazette, Oct. 27, 1804, about a letter by Jefferson: "All such doubts will be cleared up by a reference to Philip Freneau (sometime political caterer and Jackal to the author in this city)".

28. Just before this series, Joseph Lloyd in the Freeman's Journal quoted Freneau's poem, "To Shylock Ap-Shenkin" (1795 Poems, page 405), giving Freneau as the source--Aurora, May 8, 1805.

29. Editor Duane evidently had Freneau on his mind at this time--or else, helping him, Freneau instigated the reprinting, from the New York Public Advertiser, of an article, "The Tomb of the Martyrs," about the burials of prison-ship victims on the shores of Brooklyn, to which was added a quotation from Freneau's "British Prison Ship."

    The reappearance of "Juba" and "Old Soldier" (begun in the National Gazette of 1793) coincides with evidence that Freneau was in the city in the fall of 1808 and in 1809. He said, in a letter to Madison of May 12, 1809: "I have found that last winter an Edition would soon be going on...I have concluded to remain there this summer and have them published in a respectable manner"--referring to the 1809 Poems (from Madison Papers, Library of Congress). From essays in his manner in the Aurora, it seems he stayed till the spring of 1810 or later, probably as printer, writer, or assistant editor to Duane.

30. "And if Apollo does not favor him ('Weiser'), he may have recourse to Robert Slender." Who but Freneau, writing in the "Slender" or Sternesque style, would thus have referred to his pseudonymic creation? Freneau had not used it since 1801.

31. This "Soldier" series is plain and unliterary, and pretends to actual visits in Ohio and the Indian camps, but omits convincing details. The attitude toward Indians is unromantic, but otherwise sounds exactly like Freneau, who by now might have absorbed Brackenridge's realistic point of view.

32. The plain style begun by the "Old Soldier" on Dec. 12, 1811, continues in these essays; yet nearly all Freneau stood for is in them--as he had chosen to write simply as more appropriate to the plain soldier he impersonated.

33. This pseudonym was used by Freneau in FJ, Aug. 28, 1782, and was marked by him as his in his file.

34. Alexander Graydon, Memoirs of a Life, Harrisburgh, 1811.

35. This is "Americus" No. IV. No. III was omitted by the editor because "Pickering and his productions are beneath any serious criticism."

36. This contribution by "Robert Slender" is another testimony to Freneau's continued presence in the city, very likely as some sort of assistant to the Aurora editor.

37. Of the four WM essays, 1814-1817, Leary noted one, "On the Spots in the Sun," Sept. 7, 1816. By his reasoning, the two preceding ones, signed "F.", are also Freneau's. As Freneau evidently often used "L.", a letter in his Christian name and a favorite with Addison, his master, it is reasonable to ascribe "The River of Life," Sept. 20, 1817, to him.

38. In this series the "Old Soldier" reverts to Freneau's normal style, romantic and imaginative.

39. This appearance of the "Old Soldier" is the last known.

40. See P. M. Marsh, "Freneau and the Bones of Columbus," Modern Language Notes, Feb., 1945.